A Perfectionist's Guide
to <u>NOT</u> Being ~~Perfect~~

For Isaac and Todd: your love is
the most perfect thing in life.

–BZ

Books for Kids From the
American Psychological Association

Text copyright © 2022 by Bonnie Zucker. Published by Magination Press, an imprint of the American Psychological Association. All rights reserved. Except as permitted under the United States Copyright Act of 1976, no part of this publication may be reproduced or distributed in any form or by any means, or stored in a database or retrieval system, without the prior written permission of the publisher.

Magination Press is a registered trademark of the American Psychological Association. Order books at maginationpress.org, or call 1-800-374-2721.

Book design by Rachel Ross
Cover printed by Phoenix Color, Hagerstown, MD
Interior printed by Sheridan Books, Inc., Chelsea, MI

Library of Congress Cataloging-in-Publication Data
Names: Zucker, Bonnie, 1974- author.
Title: A perfectionist's guide to not being perfect / Bonnie Zucker, PsyD.
Description: Washington, DC: Magination Press, [2022] | Includes bibliographical references and index. | Audience: Ages 13-18 | Audience: Grades 10-12 | Summary: "Encourages teens to maintain their desire to achieve without striving to always be perfect and to appreciate and love who they are, not for what they accomplish"—Provided by publisher.
Identifiers: LCCN 2021043340 (print) | LCCN 2021043341 (ebook) | ISBN 9781433837036 (hardcover) | ISBN 9781433838415 (ebook)
Subjects: LCSH: Perfectionism (Personality trait) | Body image in adolescence. | Cognitive therapy for teenagers. | BISAC: YOUNG ADULT NONFICTION / Social Topics / Emotions & Feelings | YOUNG ADULT NONFICTION / Social Topics / Self-Esteem & Self-Reliance
Classification: LCC BF698.35.P47 Z83 2022 (print) | LCC BF698.35.P47 (ebook) | DDC 155.2/32—dc23
LC record available at https://lccn.loc.gov/2021043340
LC ebook record available at https://lccn.loc.gov/2021043341

Manufactured in the United States of America
10 9 8 7 6 5 4 3 2 1

A Perfectionist's Guide to <u>NOT</u> Being ~~Perfect~~

Bonnie Zucker, PsyD

MAGINATION PRESS · WASHINGTON, DC
AMERICAN PSYCHOLOGICAL ASSOCIATION

Table of Contents

Note to the Reader

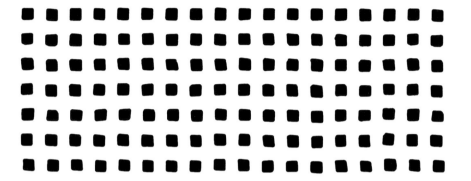

Welcome to *A Perfectionist's Guide to Not Being Perfect!* Whether this book was something you picked out, was given to you, or is something you're using as part of therapy, I hope you will find the ideas and suggestions useful and ultimately life-changing. My name is Dr. Bonnie Zucker, and I am a psychologist in private practice in Rockville, MD, just outside of Washington, D.C. I specialize in anxiety, obsessive-compulsive disorder (OCD), stress, and related issues, including perfectionism. I feel very grateful to love my work and be able to see so many young people succeed in therapy and overcome obstacles and challenges. I have met many teens with perfectionism that has caused great interference in their lives, and have watched them become free from the hold it had over them. I have also watched their self-confidence flourish as a result.

With this book, I want you to be able to achieve that, too. First, we'll talk about what perfectionism is: how it affects your life, and why you would even want to change it. First, we'll talk about the ways perfectionism may be holding you back, and what the real ingredients for a successful life are. Then we'll get to the nitty-gritty: how to challenge your perfectionism. I'll share my best tools and strategies, and give you realistic advice for finding your own way through it. We'll talk about why breaking out of your comfort zone and learning to fail are important parts of life…and can even be blessings in disguise! And finally, we'll talk about how to manage stress and live a balanced, restorative, and relaxing life.

You too can overcome perfectionism. You too can become free to live life fully, confidently, and happily, while still being accomplished and successful. That is my wish for you. Now let's begin by understanding perfectionism.

Sincerely,
Bonnie Zucker, PsyD

Chapter 1

What Is Perfectionism &
Why Change It?

66

The thing that is really hard, and
really amazing, is giving up on
being perfect and beginning the
work of becoming yourself.

-Anna Quindlen, author

Understanding the difference
between healthy striving and
perfectionism is critical to laying
down the shield and picking up
your life.

-Brené Brown, The Gifts of
Imperfection

99

It is after midnight, on a school night, and you have been seriously studying for your Spanish vocab quiz for four hours, going over your homework, reviewing your notes, and taking sample quizzes you found online. Everything you have been studying is easy—you learned it all before—but you want to be sure! It doesn't matter to you that this quiz will only count for 1% of your total grade this semester. Or that you have an A in the class (that's not even counting all the extra credit points you've accumulated). You probably wouldn't be *that* worried had you not made a mistake in the piano recital during your audition. Now more than ever your grades need to be perfect. You really want 100% on this quiz so you can guarantee your A and maintain you perfect GPA on your transcript. You have to apply for college soon. And music school is so competitive!

Or: Tennis is your passion and you've been playing since you were five years old. You've been on a school team since middle school and now, in high school, you're playing in tournaments and regularly competing as part of a university program for teens. Over the past year, it's become harder and harder to just play and enjoy your sport; instead you are in your head constantly critiquing your every stroke and beating yourself up when you miss a point. *How could you miss that? You're supposed to be better than that. This is embarrassing.* With all of these critical thoughts flowing through your head, you're not performing up to your ability. After tournaments, you watch videos of yourself playing and struggle to find anything good to focus on; it's just all about how many points you missed and how you are getting worse, not better!

Or: It's 4:00 pm and you begin getting ready for a party that starts at 7:00. Your friends are coming over at 6:00 to get you, and you need at least two hours to make yourself look right. There is no way you can leave the house unless you look perfect. Your outfit has to be ideal, your makeup needs to be perfect, your hair fully done. You start trying on clothes and it takes a full hour to figure out what to wear. Then another hour on makeup and hair. When your friends get there at 6:00, you are near tears because you hate how you look, and make them wait 30 minutes. One of them helps you change your outfit, even though she's annoyed because this happens all the time!

Perfectionism, or being a perfectionist, is something you may or may not identify with. Some people know they are perfectionists, and others don't really see themselves that way (in which case you might have been given this book by someone who thinks you should read it). We know that perfectionism exists on a spectrum, like other issues such as anxiety, ranging from mild to extreme. On the mild side, someone may spend more time than is needed checking over their work, be the very last one in the class to turn in their exam because they keep going over their answers, or keep their room spotlessly clean and organized. On the more extreme side, someone may not finish college because they couldn't complete the work on time, end friendships because others couldn't meet their extreme standards, or struggle with more significant problems such as low self-esteem, anxiety, or depression. Regardless of where you land on the spectrum, this book will help you see yourself and your accomplishments in a better light, find a better balance, and discover what goes into being a happy *and* successful person.

What Is Perfectionism?

Being a perfectionist means refusing to accept anything less than perfect. People tend to see it as a personality trait ("I'm a perfectionist" or "they are a perfectionist") that is characterized by creating and working toward excessively high, unrealistic standards that are often impossible to meet. However, lots of people think of perfectionism as a good thing, associated with high achievement, academic excellence, and intelligence. It's easy to admire perfectionists! They often seem to have their act together, and many are even complimented for working so hard. But being seen this way can become their identity, meaning that perfectionists think their achievements define who they are and are a measure of what they are worth. And this only makes the perfectionism worse!

Perfectionism can have a compulsive quality to it. You've probably heard of OCD (obsessive-compulsive disorder), which can be driven by perfectionism, but is not the same thing. OCD can involve repetitive checking, the desire for certainty, or the need for things to be "just right," which can seem similar to perfectionism. But with OCD, the thoughts and urges are experienced as intrusive and unwanted, and it's more about relieving anxiety. With perfectionism, however, the thoughts do not feel intrusive, and the person is often okay with the perfectionistic behavior, as it often seems to make their lives more organized. People with OCD would like to stop the compulsive behaviors, but it is very hard for them to do so.

Perfectionism is often about gaining the approval of others, or wanting to be accepted and admired by them, and avoiding judgment or blame. The focus then is on what others think, rather than what you think. It's a lot about wanting to be *perceived* as perfect; but this is also unattainable. Regardless of how hard you try, you cannot control the perception of others.

It's very important to realize that simply having high standards and striving to do your best isn't perfectionism. In fact, positive striving, or striving for excellence, is a good thing. When you require perfection, you feel that you must win, get the highest grade, and be the best at what you do. You are also profoundly upset and stressed by any performance or grade that's lower than your goal or what you had expected. Perfectionism is when the standards are set so high that they are out of reach, even with a great deal of effort. This sets you up for self-blame and self-criticism, which damages your self-esteem. Perfectionists have a hard time with "good enough," thinking of it as doing the bare minimum. But good enough often really *is* enough, and allowing yourself to sometimes do a good enough job lets you have more of a balanced life. The goal is to have positive striving for excellence without perfectionism and its negative consequences (such as feeling badly about yourself).

Can't Perfectionism Be a Good Thing?

There is really no such thing as "positive perfectionism," even though many perfectionists see it as a positive motivator. Perfectionism causes stress, anxiety, eating disorders, depression, and, often, exhaustion. It causes you to worry and ruminate. At the root of perfectionism is often a fear of failure, and the perfectionistic behaviors are driven by this fear. When you are afraid of trying new things because you fear that you will not be good or the best at it, or when you are so sensitive to criticism that it ruins your week, makes you pull back from others, or prevents you from taking risks and putting yourself out there, perfectionism is limiting your creativity and true self-expression. When you are constantly concerned with how you are doing and comparing yourself to others, you are unable to relax, and perfectionism is hurting you. Perfectionism prevents you from feeling good about yourself and interferes with your sense of worth. It interferes with your ability to thrive, and it becomes your *disadvantage*, not your advantage. At the end of the day, perfectionism is an obstacle to a happy and rewarding life. To quote my well-respected colleague and dear friend Dr. Mary Alvord, "People think perfectionism is a good thing. High achievement is really good; doing your best is really good. Perfectionism implies that it has to be perfect, which very few things are. It sets us up for being disappointed."

Feeling unhappy or dissatisfied with the results of your sports team tryout, audition for the school play, grade on a test, not being invited to a party, or how someone reacted to your comment in class is a common experience whether you have perfectionism or not. But perfectionists hold onto these moments, think about them as real failures, and go over them again and again in their heads. It can feel overwhelmingly stressful when you think these perceived failures cannot be undone, and that your future won't work out as you planned. This often comes from the faulty belief that perfectionistic behaviors will guarantee a good result—for example, believing that if you get all A's and excel in "your thing" (whether that's a sport, theater, or the yearbook), leads to getting into a top college, which leads to an amazing career, which leads to a happy and successful life. Perfectionism might make you believe this is the *only* path to success. So when you don't make the team, or you get a B on a test, suddenly it's like your whole life plan has been de-railed. In reality, there are *many* paths to a successful future.

Perfectionism tricks you into believing that if you just meet your very high goals and expectations, you will be satisfied and happy... but the opposite is actually true. Because these expectations can't ever be met, you end up putting forth too much effort, and then it feels even worse to not get the results you wanted. Even if the high standards of perfectionism *were* attainable, the cost of reaching them is too high, as working so much, so hard, and for so long prevents you from experiencing other important parts of life.

Perfectionism also makes failure seem like a horrible thing. So much effort is put into avoiding any failure—but believe it or not, failure is important! Someone who has never experienced occasional failures and disappointments has never had the opportunity to develop resilience and the essential coping tools that are needed later in life (since in adulthood, things don't always work out the way we'd like them to!). Becoming a successful person often depends on being able to tolerate failure and disappointment.

Perfectionism can be about school, sports, or interests. It can also be about relationships, body image and appearance, and many other areas of life. When perfectionism takes an area of your life and makes being the best the focus, not only are you less able to be present in the moment, but it also takes time away from all the other parts of life. You can't "do it all"—no one can—and the goal instead needs to be about achieving a balance so you can live a full, rewarding, and meaningful life.

When you become less perfectionistic, you will worry less about how well you are doing and what others think about your performance. You'll still try hard, but won't be as stressed or anxious about the outcome, and the outcome itself won't feel like a measure of your value as a person. You'll be able to handle the occasional "good enough" effort. You'll experience a sense of freedom that allows you to perform your best and, perhaps even more importantly, feel your best. In this book, we will be working on ways to lessen your perfectionism and the problems it is causing in your life, whether you realize how much it is impacting your wellbeing or not. And doing this will *not* interfere with your ability to do well and succeed in life—quite the opposite! It will offer you the freedom to reach your full potential.

What About School?

School deserves its own section, because it's one of the most common, and most overwhelming, areas that perfectionists struggle with. Applying yourself as a student is a wonderful trait; putting forth the effort and time it takes to do your best work is admirable. Caring about your grades, what your teachers think of you and your work, and wanting positive reflections from your peers is all good and very understandable. However, when these things are taken too far, and doing your work takes so much time that you have to miss other parts of life (socializing with friends, spending time with family, doing things that bring you joy, and taking care of your health with proper rest, nutrition, and relaxation), then your need for perfection is interfering with your life. Instead of spending time on activities that you value and make you feel good, it becomes all about excelling and achieving. It creates imbalance. The motivation becomes narrowly focused on working toward these very high goals and trying to influence how others view you.

When grades become the priority, you are also investing in a path that might not have the payoff you believe it will. You may be surprised to learn the truth about grades: academic success is actually *not* a strong predictor of career success! Academic success doesn't always reflect many of the qualities that play an important role in career and life success, like leadership, creativity, emotional intelligence, the ability to work as a team, or how well you relate and connect with others. It turns out that many highly successful people (like Albert Einstein, Steve Jobs, Whoopi Goldberg, and Dr. Martin Luther King, Jr.) did poorly in school. And many others experienced rejection in academics (Lady Gaga was teased in high school for being "too eccentric" and dropped out to pursue her career; Steven Spielberg was rejected from film school several times; actress Carey Mulligan was rejected from every drama school she applied to).

The belief that going to a top college will lead to a top career is also inaccurate. Several years ago, I read what became one of my most favorite books: *Where You Go Is Not Who You'll Be: The Antidote to the College Admissions Mania* by Frank Bruni. The book offers great advice on what college is supposed to be about: figuring out who you are, what you are about, and what you want to do with your life. In the book, Bruni quotes Anthony Carnevale, director of Georgetown University's Center on Education and the Workforce:

> "Life is something that happens slowly, and whether or not they go to their first choice [school] isn't that important. It's not the difference between Yale and jail. It's the difference between Yale and the University of Wisconsin or

some other school where they can get an excellent education. They should be thinking more about what they're going to _do_ with their lives, and what college is supposed to do is to allow you to live more fully in your time."

Bruni elaborates:

"[College is] supposed to prime you for the next chapter of learning, and for the chapter beyond that. It's supposed to put you in touch with yourself, so that you know more about your strengths, weaknesses and values and can use that information as your mooring and compass in a tumultuous, unpredictable world."

Just like the thinking about grades, it's not that you shouldn't work hard to get into a good college; it's that you shouldn't think the only way to a successful path ahead is if it starts by attending a specific college. Life does not come down to your SAT or ACT score! Working hard and getting involved in meaningful extracurricular activities, doing your best on your college essays, and getting good grades is a solid approach to getting into college. But what you do *in* college, and what you discover about yourself, will take you further than simply graduating from a top school. College is also about the relationships you nurture and what you learn about yourself in those relationships; that plays a very meaningful role in determining what your post-college "adult" life will look like. Time magazine published a great article written by my colleague, Dr. Bill Stixrud, titled "It's time to tell your kids it doesn't matter where they go to college." In the article, he clarifies that success, as measured by income and job and life satisfaction, is not determined by going to an elite college or a state university. He explains that success comes from both working hard at something we enjoy *and* being able to recover when things don't work out for us.

I'm not encouraging you to not care about academics, but I am hoping you will think differently about grades, and if you are overly attached to them, perhaps loosen that attachment. See grades for what they are—and they are not everything. Your grades and academic success do not determine how far you will go in life. *Who* you are, not what you've accomplished, or what your report card looks like, or how many awards you have earned, or how perfectly in shape you are, matters the most, and your ability to connect with and relate to others will take you much further in life than you think.

The same applies to sports and other extracurricular activities: wanting to do your best and be recognized in your area is fantastic, but when you take it to such a high level that you are never satisfied, lose the excitement or fun of doing it, or constantly self-criticize, then perfectionism has taken over. Perfectionism makes it all about performance, ranking, and winning, and drains the joy from things you used to love. It is possible to be a great athlete or performer, love participating, be really, really good (not necessarily the best), and be happy with your teammates and the bonds with them (which really matters even more). What if we consider that this might be what winning really means? Perhaps winning at life is more about finding balance and living a full experience, unlimited by the confines of perfectionism.

How Do I Recognize Perfectionism?

In order to understand perfectionism better, let's look at its symptoms and impact, along with some examples. Sometimes it can be hard to see yourself as separate from the perfectionism, because it feels like this is who you are, and it can feel natural to have these standards. Take a look at this list and see which apply to you:

Signs of Perfectionism:

- Refusing to accept anything less than perfect
- Holding yourself to impossible-to-meet high standards
- Believing your worth is measured by your achievements or grades
- Being hyper-focused on grades
- Needing to get straight As or be the best at your sport/chosen activity
- Spending excessive amounts of time on projects or schoolwork because you have to make it perfect
- Checking work over and over again
- Needing extensions to hand in assignments or papers
- Being preoccupied with rules and lists
- Being rigid and inflexible (for example, if plans change)
- Having difficulty asking for help
- Having difficulty delegating tasks to others
- Having difficulty making decisions
- Procrastinating

- Being unable to handle making a mistake
- Feeling guilty for a mistake or perceived failures
- Being self-critical and harsh with yourself if your performance falls short of perfect
- Constantly comparing yourself to others
- Being happy only when you win
- Being unable to accept feedback or constructive criticism
- Spending hours on your appearance
- Refusing to leave the house unless you look your best
- Hyper-focusing on parts of your body that you are not happy with
- Having negative body-image because your body is not perfect
- Being critical of others, often feeling disappointed by them
- Restricting your eating (for example, wanting to stay within a certain calorie range, only eating 100% clean foods, keeping weight the same number, eating only when you've achieved a goal, etc.)
- Waking up very early at the same time every day to exercise for a set amount of time (which is usually excessive, like two hours)
- Expecting that others won't make mistakes
- Finding it hard to be happy for others when they do well
- Having trouble sharing your thoughts or feelings
- Finding it difficult to relax and let go
- Being unable to be spontaneous
- Being unwilling to try new things because you won't immediately be good at them

Impact of Perfectionism:

- Stress
- Low self-esteem/self-worth
- Low self-confidence (not believing in yourself)
- Self-doubt
- Self-criticism
- Feeling lots of pressure
- Feeling like a failure
- Guilt
- Shame
- Inability to celebrate your achievements
- Negative impact on relationships with parents, teachers, friends, etc.
- Anxiety
- Depression
- Exhaustion or fatigue
- Trouble being close to others because you are overly judgmental
- Others perceiving you as judgmental or "hard" on them
- Limited problem-solving skills because of inflexible thinking
- Limited creativity (from trying to please others)
- Missing out on fun experiences
- Missing out on being social
- Physical problems such as gastrointestinal issues and headaches
- Body image disturbance
- Eating disorders
- Feeling suicidal

Examples of Perfectionism:

- Studying for four hours for a quiz that counts for 1% of your grade.
- Arguing with the teacher for the extra 4% after receiving a 96% on a paper.
- Putting off writing a paper because thinking about how it had to be perfect made it seem overwhelming, and then having to ask for an extension.

- Being unwilling to try a new kickboxing class because you're afraid of not being good at it.

- Giving up after going to three tennis practices because you don't think you're as good as the other players.

- Yelling at your friend for picking you up 15 minutes late, and being unable to let it go for an hour.

- Refusing to eat any cake (not even a bite) at a birthday party because you don't want to have any sugar.

- Thinking over and over and over about the wrong answer you gave in class, and how the person next to you got it right.

Do any of these sound like you? If so, think about the impact they're having on your life. How do they influence how you feel and act?

Types of Perfectionism

There are many different types of perfectionism. It can be general perfectionism, which is mostly about wanting things to be a certain way, or it can focus on something specific like academics, sports, relationships with friends and family, or body image. It can come out as being rigid and inflexible, and oriented to the rules: for example, when you feel continually disappointed by others. Or it can be something more internal and hidden, where it's more about judging and criticizing yourself in a harsh manner: for example, constantly ruminating over things that made you feel guilty. Some perfectionists come across as people-pleasers, while others are difficult and argumentative.

Check out this breakdown of some examples:

General	Wanting things to be a certain way, rigidity/inflexibility, closed to change. Being self-critical, judging yourself. Ruminating over mistakes.
Academic	Requiring top grades/all As. Arguing for extra points.
Sports performance	Requiring excelling in sports: always starting, being the best player, etc.
Body image	Strictly pursuing a certain body type, often thin and toned or lean and muscular.
Relationships	Holding others to high standards and not being forgiving or flexible if others make mistakes or do things in a different way. Judging others.
People-pleasing	Prioritizing what others think of you, saying "yes" and being agreeable even when it's not your preference. Putting others' needs and preferences above your own.

Where Does It Come From?

While the causes of perfectionism are different for everyone, there are some common themes, like:

- fear of disappointing or upsetting others,
- perfectionistic parents or other important people,
- competitive environment,
- fear of failure or not measuring up (being inadequate), or
- early loss or trauma.

The pressure to be perfect may be coming from you; the comparisons you make with others (peers, siblings); from your parents, coaches, and teachers; or from a competitive environment. You may have adults who criticize you (even when you do well), don't compliment or celebrate you, expect perfection, or compare you to others, such as high-achieving siblings. The environment can be an academically rigorous school or a very competitive ballet company, dance, swim, or wrestling team that promotes perfection. In these situations, you may need to work to separate yourself from the values that are part of these systems that influence you. And some people who have had a loss or trauma and endured something outside of their control may become perfectionistic as a means of coping and gaining a sense of control in their lives. Regardless of the cause, it can be improved. Regardless of whose fault it is, it is up to you to change it. And you can do it!

What Do You Want to Achieve?

When you are perfectionistic, you end up creating a small comfort zone for yourself. Anything less than perfect falls outside of that comfort zone, like trying new things or sticking with something that doesn't come easily or naturally. Making mistakes, accepting blame, or losing a game can all fall outside of it as well. With a small comfort zone comes an unwillingness to put yourself out there, which prevents you from developing resilience (we'll discuss resilience and other building blocks for a successful, happy future in adulthood in the next chapter). Finally, the wisest people are often the most flexible in their thinking, have strong self-awareness, keep the bigger picture in mind, and use common sense and compassion when seeing and understanding the world. You can't do any of these things if you're constantly focused on being perfect.

So let's consider the goal of reading this book. Why read it? While everyone will have different specific goals and their own personal experience with perfectionism, the big-picture theme is to challenge yourself to be more flexible in the way you approach certain areas of your life. When you lower your expectations for yourself or even just show some flexibility, you create more opportunity to feel proud and happy with your performance. The goal is to take pride in your work and in doing it well, enjoy the process of doing projects, participate in interests that you are passionate about, and celebrate your achievements. The goal is to maintain your desire to accomplish and achieve without striving to always be perfect. The goal is to appreciate and love yourself for who you are, not for what you do or achieve. The goal is to find balance between work and play. Without play and downtime to just be, you are at risk of losing your energy for life, not being able to identify or further develop your passions, and not being nearly as creative.

Finally, it may sound silly, but challenging your perfectionism is also about the pursuit of happiness. It's hard to be happy when you've created a very narrow window of what defines success. It's hard to be happy when you always put your work first, without making room for being with friends and having fun. It's hard to be happy when you feel a lot of pressure or are making harsh, critical comments about yourself. Believe it or not, you'll find that when you are happy, you do your best work. Happiness has its own energy, and that energy will free you to fully thrive. People will also be drawn to you by your good energy and positive outlook. Your most creative self will emerge from happiness. It already exists within you; you just need to clear out the limits of perfectionism to fully experience it.

When you can recognize that perfectionism is a disadvantage, you can become motivated to do something about it. For many people, it may just be shifting the perfectionism a bit to land in a more positive place. It might be about deciding when and where to be slightly perfectionistic and when it's okay to simply do a "good enough" job on something. It might be about learning how to be more flexible in general. You can learn to tweak your perfectionistic habits and behaviors without feeling like your identity is threatened. You will still be you, just a you who is more free, more flexible, more confident, and happier.

So let's get ready to make some shifts!

FROM:	→	TO:
Perfection	→	Positive striving
Self-criticism	→	Self-compassion
Rigidity	→	Flexibility
Avoiding risks	→	Willing to take reasonable risks
Small comfort zone	→	Expanded comfort zone

In this book, you will learn the strategies and tools needed to make these shifts, and to try out a different way of thinking and behaving. As you do, you will discover many positive things about yourself and how you want to be in the world.

Chapter 1
In A Nutshell:

- Perfectionism is when you refuse to accept anything less than perfect, and it's a disadvantage (not an advantage). It can cause stress, anxiety, eating disorders, and depression, and limits you from trying new things and feeling good about yourself.

- Perfectionism makes you fear failure and see only one path to being successful in life (even though there are many paths!).

- Perfectionism and positive striving for excellence are not the same thing.

- Grades are not everything!

- Perfectionism can manifest in many ways. But no matter the type or cause of your perfectionism, you can work to change it!

Chapter 2

What Makes a Successful Life?

66 "If you're curious, you'll never be bored. The world will open up to you over and over."

-Reese Witherspoon, actress

"The two most important days in your life are the day you are born and the day you discover the reason why."

-Mark Twain, author

"My mother instilled in me the idea that creativity starts with a leap of faith—telling your fears they are not allowed where you are headed."

-Beyoncé, musical artist **99**

Perfectionists are usually very invested in their (rigid) way of doing things, based on the belief that it will ensure a good result. After all, why devote all of this effort to getting the best grades if it doesn't get you into a top college? Why practice for your audition hours and hours more than anyone else if it doesn't land you the lead role? Why spend so much time creating the perfect Instagram page if it doesn't get the most likes? It's also easy to get attached to our habits and ways of doing things. But when it comes to success, perfectionism doesn't offer as much as you might think. As discussed in the first chapter, perfectionism limits your comfort zone, hinders creativity, promotes a fear of failure that leads to avoidance of trying new things and taking risks, and can lead to stress, anxiety, and depression, among other problems. It's also clear that academic success or even where you go to college is not predictive of life or career success, so making your grades your number one priority in your life is not the best approach. But if grades are not the answer, and being the very best isn't the answer to being successful in life, then what is? Well, new research has been finding out!

Some of the actual main factors related to success are:

Self-Compassion

People who have self-compassion (versus self-criticism) are more successful. Perfectionists may struggle more than most with self-compassion because they hold themselves to super high standards, often ones that are impossible to meet. Perfectionism lays the foundation for self-criticism; when you don't reach your (unrealistically high) goals, you might call yourself names and mentally beat yourself up with self-deprecating comments. That inner critic can really hurt your sense of worth.

As humans, we feel threatened by harsh criticism and shame, and this activates the "flight-or-fight" part of our brain, called the amygdala. When you are kind to yourself, you brain calms down and works more efficiently. In order for the part of your brain that is good at thinking and analyzing (the prefrontal cortex) to work at its best, the amygdala cannot be activated. Having self-compassion means showing understanding and kindness to yourself; it's the opposite of being critical and demanding of yourself. Dr. Kristin Neff, the lead researcher on self-compassion and author of *Self-Compassion: The Proven Power of Being Kind to Yourself,* explains that self-compassion has three parts:

1. self-kindness: being gentle and understanding with yourself, rather than being critical, harsh, and judgmental.
2. common humanity: when you acknowledge how there is a universal experience of life that everyone has; it's the opposite of feeling alone in your struggles.
3. mindfulness: when you are aware of your experience and you acknowledge it without denying your pain.

Self-Kindness

It's useful to think of self-kindness as a nurturing practice you can use, especially when you're struggling. Show understanding and kindness in your self-talk by empathizing with yourself and your situation. Self-talk comments such as "it's okay I'm feeling this way right now," and "this is a really stressful project and it's just taking a while" will offer a sense of inner support. Self-compassion can help you regulate your emotions better. Self-kindness involves comforting yourself and being patient, nurturing, and understanding with yourself, especially when things don't work out the way you'd hoped. Those are the times when you most need to support yourself with kindness.

You can acknowledge how upsetting it is, validate your feelings of disappointment, and then follow it with self-love, self-soothing, and recognizing that everyone fails at some point.

Common Humanity

Although some perfectionists hold others to their same impossible-to-meet standards and often end up feeling disappointed in or annoyed by them, most still find it easier to be kind to and forgiving of others, especially friends. This is the "common humanity" part of having self-compassion. It's also important to see that there is a universal experience to having a bad day, going through a rough patch, or not getting the outcome you really wanted and worked hard for. The opposite of this would be taking it personally—where you make it about you, as if you are the only one not able to achieve, or you see your failure as evidence that *you* are a failure.

Mindfulness

When you are mindful, you are able to recognize your feelings with awareness and you can sit with your negative feelings (disappointment, anger, shame, etc.) without minimizing or exaggerating them. By sitting with your feelings and not trying to avoid them or react to them (which often makes it worse), you give your emotions the space they need, allowing them to settle down. With perfectionism, it feels natural to ruminate and obsess about mistakes or failures, and this leads to feeling terrible about yourself or to a sense of embarrassment and shame. When you learn to be mindful, you can see these feelings for what they are (the result of perfectionism), rather than letting them feed into a negative view of yourself. As an observer of your thoughts, you can see your thoughts as just thoughts and not become too attached to them.

Take a moment to think about a time when you either failed at something or did not perform as well as you'd have liked. How did you handle it? What messages did you give yourself (in your self-talk)?

For example, imagine you got an A- on a biology exam and felt it was really going to mess up your report card. Do you tend to say *I should have worked harder, what's wrong with me?* Or something more supportive like, *It will be okay, I can recover from this, and it was great that I put so much into studying.* Instead of being judgmental with yourself, and saying something like *I am so stupid. I can't get anything right,* try replacing it with *I have to be loving with myself. I am trying so hard and it's okay if I don't get 100%. I believe in myself!* The same is true if you tend to be judgmental of others. Instead of thinking *What's wrong with her?* try thinking *Maybe she's having a hard time today.* Believe it or not, when you cultivate nonjudging energy, even if it's towards others, it brings more peace and calmness into your life. This helps things not feel so intense.

So try being kinder and gentler with yourself. Many perfectionists believe they need to push themselves hard and be tough on themselves to get the best effort. This is not true, and there is no evidence to support it. All the evidence actually supports cultivating self-compassion. Self-compassion offers a way of soothing and balancing yourself, which allows you to perform and feel your best.

Grab a pen and paper and write **3-5 encouraging self-compassionate statements** that you can use when facing a challenge.

A self-compassionate voice sounds like: *I will be kind to myself. It's okay that this happened. I can fix it and recover. I'm okay and it's going to be fine. It's okay to feel what I feel. Everyone... (makes mistakes, is not perfect, fails—whatever the situation may be).*

Self-Confidence

Self-confidence just means you believe in yourself and your ability to accomplish a goal. It means you trust yourself to figure it out and make it work. When you think about your past performance and what you were able to accomplish, your self-confidence becomes stronger. You can then lean on that sense of confidence as you put your energy into new tasks and goals. It's often confused with self-esteem, but self-esteem is one's sense of self-worth or self-worthiness, which is a little different. While it's great to have solid self-esteem (especially in social relationships, as it protects you against tolerating being treated poorly by others), and you want to know your value, it is not as big a predictor for success.

Believing in your ability to succeed (self-confidence) is more important. Self-compassion ties in here as well, because if you have self-compassion you'll be more likely to reach your goals, and that will increase your confidence about meeting future goals. Self-confidence will also allow you to take more risks, which is an important part of life (we will look more into taking healthy risks in Chapter 9). When you believe in yourself, you will feel better and be happier.

Grab a pen and paper and write **3-5 self-confident statements** you can use when facing a challenge. Even if you don't believe them right now—just saying them can still help.

When you work toward a goal from a place of happiness, you will feel motivated and energized.

A self-confident voice sounds like: *I can do this. I've got this! I believe I am good at this and will get it. It will work out for me. I've done well before and I can do it again.*

Internal Locus of Control

An internal locus of control is the belief that you can affect the circumstance of your life, or at least your experience of it. A person with an internal locus of control looks at a difficult situation and thinks *what can I do to impact this, what is my role in changing this,* or, *how can I see this differently so it's not that hard to deal with?* A person with an *external* locus of control believes that the control is outside of them; that no matter what they do, outside factors (like the situation around you, other people's actions, or luck) matter more in terms of the outcome. When you are faced with a challenge, the goal is to focus on what you *can* do to change it, not all the reasons you can't.

Internal locus of control is a key factor in coping well throughout life. It allows you to be an agent of change in your life and know that you can get things done. You know what is within your control and make that your focus, and ask

> Think about a situation where you felt overwhelmed and helpless. In hindsight, is there something you could've done to make it better, or at least change your experience of it?

for help when needed. No matter how hard the situation, there is something you can do to improve it.

An internal locus of control voice sounds like: *There is something I can do to change this. I can take action and change the situation for myself!*

Growth Mindset

Are you good at math? Bad at sports? Did you ever think these things could change? Turns out, it's all about your mindset.

The idea of mindset was most famously researched by a psychologist named by Dr. Carol Dweck, who described two very different mindsets: growth and fixed. People with a fixed mindset believe they have a predetermined (and fixed) amount of intelligence, skill, or talent. This belief often leads to giving up and not putting effort into tasks that do not come naturally. They don't think they can get better, so why bother trying? It can come up in other ways, including ones that can really hurt you. For example, if you have a negative body image and think to yourself *if I can't have my ideal body, I won't ever be happy*, you end up getting locked in this mindset with no way out. Or you really want to play a sport, but because you've never done it before, you assume you will never be good enough and don't even try. This type of mindset is a lot like "all-or-nothing" thinking, which we'll discuss in Chapter 6.

With a growth mindset, however, people see intelligence and abilities as things that can change over time; you become smarter as you grow and, with effort and persistence, you can become very, very good at something. In a growth mindset, since intelligence, skill, and talent can be acquired, failure and effort are understood as ways of acquiring more intelligence and experience, and you are more likely to stick with it. Plus, when you can overcome setbacks, you learn what you are really capable of, and your self-confidence goes up. Meanwhile, people with a fixed mindset have a tendency towards all-or-nothing thinking, giving up easily, and having their identity wrapped up in how good they are at doing something. If they cannot achieve something, they feel completely defeated and are at risk of losing their sense of self. In the very worst cases, it can even lead to depression.

What's something you weren't very good at when you started, but have gotten better at over time?

A growth mindset voice sounds like: *I will keep working at this and figure it out. I don't need to get it on the first try, I need to stay with it. If I keep putting in the effort and trying hard, I will learn and I will succeed.*

Grit

Grit is the willingness to stick with a task; *stick-with-it-ness*. Researchers have found that grit is actually more predictive of success than intelligence. You can be the smartest person in the world, but if you don't try hard, work at it, and stick with it, you're not likely to succeed. Grit has two parts: passion and perseverance. It is important that you figure out what you are passionate about and let that drive you; put your efforts into your passions and into enjoying them (*not* how well you are doing them). Perseverance is not giving up, even in the face of obstacles. Grit involves having some mental toughness, where you can overcome obstacles and end up being stronger as a result.

A gritty voice sounds like: *I won't give up. I will stick with this and persevere. Nothing can stop me!*

Resilience

Resilience is being able to handle whatever comes your way: in other words, being able to navigate through obstacles and come out on top. And like all of these, it can be learned! Resilience makes you less likely to have mental health problems, including anxiety and depression. A rigid, inflexible style of thinking (like perfectionism), makes it harder to consider different paths to take; it seems like there is one way of doing things, one best result, one right outcome. But people with resilience will find a new way of looking at a situation, will problem-solve and not let anything stand in their way of going after a goal. Because of this, they also develop more grit. People with resilience are good at problem-solving; they don't avoid asking for help, they can call on their support system, and are better able to handle disappointment. We will specifically focus on tolerating disappointment and making mistakes in Chapter 9.

Think of a time when you were faced with a challenge, something that wasn't natural for you or didn't come easily. Did you stick with it or give up?

A resilient voice sounds like: *I can handle whatever comes my way! It won't knock me down!*

Self-Efficacy

Self-efficacy is a more specific type of self-confidence. It relates to your belief in how capable you are of doing a specific task. People with high self-efficacy are more likely to get started on a project. For example, when a student with high self-efficacy gets an assignment for a class and says to themselves *"I can do this in a week,"* the ideas start pouring in. Perfectionism can interfere with this because the task may become overly complicated or detailed, or the pressure to make it perfect can interfere with that sense of "I can do it," or "I've got this." Perfectionism often makes the assignment feel like it's a measure of intelligence or knowledge, rather than acknowledging that the assignment is about learning and figuring it out. It may feel like it has to be the most scholarly work and feels like a burden. When it feels like it will require a lot of effort because it has to be perfect, getting started can be hard. This is why perfectionism can lead to procrastination. If perfectionism is the driving factor, it's the drive to excel, prove yourself, or be the best

Do you have a tendency to procrastinate? If so, can you think of some self-efficacy statements you could use to get started?

in the class. With the focus on these things, the joy of doing the assignment, the reward of gaining knowledge, and the sense of "I've got this" gets missed.

A self-efficacy voice sounds like: *I know I can get this done. It won't take that long!*

Delay of Gratification

Delaying gratification just means you're willing to wait for a reward. Sounds simple, but it can be a hard skill! The most famous study on this was actually with really young kids: "The Marshmallow Test" study tested whether preschoolers were able to resist the temptation to eat one marshmallow (or another favorite dessert, like a cookie) in front of them in order to get *two* later. The study then followed those kids over a 40-year period and found that the preschoolers who delayed gratification at the young age showed more self-control as teenagers when they were frustrated or faced with temptation, and were more focused, intelligent, and confident. As adults, these preschoolers who delayed gratification ended up having higher education levels, had fewer weight problems, and showed more resilience when it came to dealing with relationship problems. While there's some debate about how accurate this study actually was (the researchers may not have taken enough other factors about the kids' lives into consideration when looking at their success later in life), being able to delay gratification is definitely a good thing, and the marshmallow test *also* showed it could be learned. In the study, some kids who were not able to resist the first marshmallow even for a few seconds at first were able to learn to wait for the better reward after being taught a few strategies.

As a perfectionist, you might be well-practiced at delaying gratification...or you might not be, as some perfectionists can't wait to check something off their list, or might be in a hurry to get a result and rush through tasks. Walter Mischel, the author of *The Marshmallow Test* (a book about the study), explains that delaying gratification involves learning how to distract yourself from the temptation in front of you and activating what he calls "the cool system". The cool system is essentially using the prefrontal cortex, where your reasoning skills come from. The "hot system" is the amygdala, which is where emotions come from. It's the hot system which makes it hard to delay gratification.

Funny story: years ago, I became addicted to blueberry scones. I'm generally a very healthy eater, but I got used to having one every morning with my coffee. I wanted to stop eating them *every* day because they are processed and have little nutritional value. If I thought about the warmed-up scone with my hot coffee, and the delicious combination of the two, my "hot system" would be fully peaked and I'd order the scone. I decided to activate my "cool system" and planned to pretend that the blueberries were cockroaches (disgusting, I know—I went a little far with it as I was really motivated). Each time I approached the counter at the coffee shop and saw those delicious scones, I would cue myself: *those are cockroaches in there, not blueberries. Cockroaches!* and would distract myself by thinking of other things (like making lists of cities, states, and countries using the alphabet:

Aventura,
Bethesda,
Chicago,
Denmark,
Ecuador,
Florida,
Georgia,
Hawaii,
Italy...).

Sure enough, I was able to stop ordering them. It actually worked! Months went by without eating them, and then the psychologist in me was curious about what would happen if I tried to eat one. So, one day I ordered it: a warmed-up blueberry scone with coffee. I sat down and took one bite of the corner piece (without any blueberries in it) and I couldn't eat any more than that! It literally changed the way I thought about and experienced scones.

Mostly, this strategy involves changing the way something is mentally represented. For perfectionists, the "gratification" can actually be the need to finish or perfect a task. But if you are able to think about it differently and even distract yourself, you will find that you can delay it. With practice, you can learn to not react so quickly, and develop a new pattern or habit.

A delay of gratification voice sounds like: *I don't need to have every single thing done in order to have a fun break. I can hold off and wait to... (check, ask, or get reassurance).*

Creativity

Finally, creativity is essential. Creativity can come in many forms, but the idea here is to allow yourself to fully express yourself, without the barriers and limits that come from trying to do something to fit someone else's ideals (which perfectionism encourages). If your efforts are focused on pleasing others and having them perceive you in a certain way, you shift into a place that is essentially the opposite of creativity. When you allow yourself to be creative, you are aligning with what you see, think, and feel—like how when you express yourself artistically, it's about your perception. Others may like it or not; personal preference for art varies a great deal. But when your happiness and joy come from being able to engage in the creative process, so many amazing things can come from that. Cultivating creativity requires you to free yourself from the excessively high standards you have set for yourself or that you are letting others set for you.

Coming up with different solutions to problems also requires creativity. Thinking outside the box, seeing an issue from different angles, and considering alternatives are all ways of being creative.

A creative voice sounds like: *I can come up with another solution! There are so many ways of doing something.*

You can see how these nine concepts are all quite related. Self-compassion leads to more self-confidence. Self-confidence supports a growth mindset, and a growth mindset supports internal locus of control, which supports resilience, which supports grit. If your perfectionism leads to a fixed mindset, you will not try as hard, not develop the self-confidence you need to work at problems, and this will interfere with growing your grittiness, which will interfere with your resilience. Delaying gratification also grows your confidence, as does having high self-efficacy. Creativity also helps make you more resilient and can boost your sense of an internal locus of control. They are all connected. Try to think about which of these factors you need to work on the most. Be proud of yourself for working on them: self-improvement is something to feel good about!

Chapter 2
In A Nutshell:

- Perfectionism is not the key to a successful life.

- The nine factors related to success in life are: self-compassion, self-confidence, internal locus of control, growth mindset, grit, resilience, self-efficacy, delay of gratification, and creativity.

- All of these factors are inter-related; working on any one will help grow the others!

- A lot of them boil down to believing in yourself, speaking kindly to yourself, not giving up, and pushing through challenges.

Chapter 3

Picture Perfect: Social Media

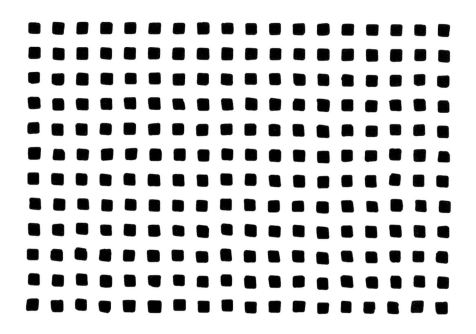

"

"I think imperfections are important, just as mistakes are important. You only get to be good by making mistakes, and you only get to be real by being imperfect."

-Julianne Moore, actress

"

Appearance is such a loaded concept. Worrying about how we look—both physically and in the image of the life we project to the world—is an extremely common struggle. Nearly everyone worries about this in some way! But for people with perfectionism, it can be overwhelming.

This and the next chapter will focus on struggles with feelings about appearance. Sometimes being overly preoccupied with how you look can lead to serious problems like depression or an eating disorder, but more often it leads to just spending a lot of time and energy focusing on your appearance. Often, there is a sense of not feeling satisfied or confident in yourself and how you look. This is fueled by comparing yourself to others, which often results in you feeling badly about yourself.

This can feel like a lot of pressure and can sometimes lead you to behave in ways that don't truly reflect *who* you are or what you are about. It can also create people-pleasing behavior. How you act becomes more about how you would *like* to be, or about winning the approval of others, rather than what actually makes you happy.

Constructing Reality

Social media is one of the main ways that comparisons are made. Before we look into the downside of social media, I want to say that technology isn't a bad thing. The opportunities offered by technology are endless—it's really amazing. It can foster connection with others, encourage creativity, be a source of entertainment, and you can learn a great deal about a lot of things. Yet, there are also a lot of problems that come from technology, and from social media in particular. Though you might enjoy your own profile and sharing pictures, it is important to recognize that everything you post is *constructed*. It is something you created. It's the perspective on your life that you want to put out there, for others to see. The same is true for others. Though the photos are real, usually people only post their best ones, or even use a filter. Their posts show them at their best, and typically make their lives look fun and problem-free. When something is constructed, it is created with a certain goal in mind. In the case of social media posts, the goal is usually to look good and portray a wonderful life. It's not an accurate reflection of reality, though, because it's only an isolated part of it; it's not the whole story. One's posts usually don't show them at moments when they are struggling with hard emotions, or having trouble getting something done, or fighting with their family or friends, or when they just woke up in the morning or are getting over a cold. The goal of looking good, looking like you are having a great time, and so on, is the frame by which these pictures get posted. There is a need to present oneself in a certain way that has a lot to do with getting approval from others (literally, in the form of likes and comments). In many ways, doing this implies that just being you is not good enough, and can foster a feeling of inadequacy.

In addition, in situations where you see others having so much fun with friends or going to events, it can create a fear of missing out and a belief that others are enjoying life more than you. Some studies have found that most people think other's social lives are better than their own. Specifically, they found that most of the participants believed their friends went to more parties than they did, had more friends, ate out more, and had better social lives. One study found that college students are experiencing more perfectionism than in the past, and the researchers suggested it might be due to social media. Another found that teens who spend three or more hours a day on social media had a higher rate of mental health problems, including anxiety and depression.

There isn't anything wrong with going to an event and posting a picture, but what comes from it is often not so simple. While no one is always happy or perfect, scrolling through the photos and videos of friends and celebrities where everyone looks their best and seems to be having an amazing time can lead to negative feelings about yourself or your own life. It's easy to get caught up in how great others look and what they are doing, and to take this as evidence that you are not having as good of a time. It's easy to believe that is how their life is *all* the time and not recognize that those pictures and great times are balanced out by imperfections, struggles, and not-always-so-positive emotions. It's easy to look at those perfect photos and conclude that the people in them don't have any issues or problems. But the truth is they are just as stressed and at times anxious and emotional as the rest of us. Everyone has moments of self-doubt and stress; no one is free from struggles or obstacles. But looking at posts, especially when you're selecting the ones that you are most drawn to, can feed the image of the life you want. The posts you admire (that may create feelings of jealously) can become what you see as the goal for how a fulfilling, exciting, and attractive life should look.

The same is true of ads with models or stories about celebrities in lifestyle publications: the images you see shape what you think is ideal. Models appear to have the perfect bodies: whether it's skinny and tall or having perfect abs and lean muscles. Everyone, no matter sex or gender, is affected by these beauty standards. But many times, these images have been airbrushed, taken with a filter, or just plain edited. Again, these images of others looking "perfect" are constructed. We often find out that photos are not the whole story: for example, celebrity couples who announce a break-up a few days after they were photographed looked very happy and close. This is what a photo is: it's just an image of a very particular moment in time. Sometimes it's true, sometimes it's not. Sometimes it's the whole story, sometimes it's just a small part of the story. Maybe those abs are real, but at what cost did the person get them? It's important to remember this when seeing other's photos and stories. It's important not to get too caught up in it all.

Take a moment to consider how social media makes you feel. Write it down: maybe it's positive (connected, entertained, informed) or negative (bad about self/ appearance, insecure, FOMO, not as popular), or a combination of both.

You might also consider:

- What are the advantages and disadvantages for you?
- Who do you admire on social media because they are authentic and don't always look "perfect" or "put together"?

One challenge I like to suggest is to go on a "Social Media Diet" for a day (or even just a part of a day if a full day is too much for you), week, or month. Then you can write about your experience: How did it feel? Were you anxious and stressed or less stressed and carefree? What did you do with the free time from not being on social media?

Pressure to Post

There can be a pressure to post as well, almost a feeling like if it happened, there should be a post about it. I once heard from a 15-year-old girl who said she and her friends were sick of having to constantly post on Instagram and Snapchat. It started to feel like a burden. She shared that one night she and about 14 friends all got together for a small party. Everyone was looking at their phones when someone said they wished they could all just be together without screens. Another friend agreed and suggested they all put them in another room for the evening. For the rest of the night, without their phones, no one took even one photo. It was a great night; everyone was so relaxed that they really bonded. The next week in school, another friend asked her about her weekend and she shared what she did; he looked confused and commented that he hadn't seen any pictures of it. When she told him about the no-phones thing, he was amazed and said something about how next time he wanted to be included because it was even cooler that no one knew about it. When she told me about this, we laughed, because we knew he thought it was this hard-to-get-into secret party, when it was actually the most chill evening for them.

This also brings up what posting actually means for you. What happens to a picture or an event when you post it? How does it change that photo for you? There are photos that are so special to me, usually of my kids, that I would never post. Not because of privacy, not because of how I look or how they look, but because there are some things so sacred that I don't want them to be compromised by the opinions of others. Even if those opinions and comments are purely positive, it ultimately takes away from it being just mine. With the vulnerability that comes from exposing it to the world to comment on, it becomes less sacred.

> Do you have a favorite photo you would like just for yourself?

Social Comparisons

We easily become so reliant on the posts people make and the photos they share. That's just how the world works right now! But I will caution you: when you look at these things through the lens of perfectionism, it will (falsely) become evidence that you are not measuring up, don't look as good, aren't as fit, aren't having as great of a time, and aren't succeeding as much as others. Perfectionism breeds social comparisons; because you are so preoccupied with how well you are doing, you'll naturally look at others to see how you compare. These "normative comparisons" (when you compare yourself to others) are the problem. With perfectionism "relative comparisons" (when you compare yourself to yourself) can also be a problem, as you can feel you are not doing as well as you could do or have done in the past—but they are still preferable to normative ones. Also, you can work with relative comparisons to make it an advantage, especially when you add in self-compassion and gratitude. For example: am I becoming better at slowing down and feeling gratitude for my life and all I have, even the small things? Am I prioritizing my mental well-being more often by taking time to relax?

In some ways, we can blame this tendency to compare on the fact that you are given grades at school: it sets you up for comparisons. But as you grow up and enter into adulthood, this grading system doesn't exist. You can still compare yourself to others, but an external system of evaluation usually doesn't play a role (except in some jobs where you are ranked, such as "top salesperson" in the company). Take my work, for example: when I see someone for a therapy session, we have our meeting, connect with each other, I usually teach them strategies, we work together to decide what things to work on over the week, and we warmly say good-bye. There is no comparison to anyone else—it's just about the time we spent together. It's not like there is some evaluator watching the session from a two-way mirror who evaluates me and compares me to other psychologists!

When it comes to preventing comparisons, the goal is to be more present in the moment, focus on what you are doing at the time you are doing it, and pay attention to how you feel about what you are doing. That's it. There are (ideally) no comparisons in your head or in real life. The goal is to be happy and grateful for who you are, for what is amazing about you, for what you have, for what you are doing, for your relationships, and your passions. When it comes down to it, making comparisons is never a winning situation: you will always find someone smarter, stronger, who has won more awards, reached higher goals, has more friends, placed higher than you did, is skinnier or more muscular or fit, has better clothes, etc. Wanting what everyone else has (or seems to have) takes the focus away from your own life. It takes the focus away from what *you* have and leads to feelings of deprivation.

There is no such thing as perfect; we have to live life with appreciation and gratitude and focus on what we want to achieve and accomplish (in a healthy, non-perfectionistic way). The goal is: *less constructing and more living.* When you live this way, you will be your happiest self. Comparisons are *not* the path to happiness and well-being. They are set up to leave you feeling "less than" and perhaps even lead to low self-esteem and depression.

Comparisons can also interfere with relationships and your ability to really connect and relate to peers. When you view others through the lens of comparison, you're constantly either thinking about how they're in a better or worse place than you, neither of which will allow for a real connection or relationship to flourish. You're focusing on standing rather than who they are as a person. The same is true for siblings. If you are in constant comparison with your brother or sister, whether it's about achievements, grades, athletics, number of friends, appearance, or whatever, those

Is there someone you know you tend to compare yourself to? It could be someone from your real-life, or a celebrity. Do these comparisons make you feel better, or worse?

comparisons can compromise the warmth and connection you have or could have.

It's essential to see that someone else's success and achievements say nothing about you. If your sibling or friend excels in something, just admire them. Love them for being great at what they do. Be proud of them for their hard work and efforts. Admire them for being so good, strong, successful, attractive. Then you will not only connect beautifully with them, you will have another thing to love about yourself: your good, humble nature and a strong sense of confidence and self-esteem. When you are confident and know your self-worth, nothing is a threat to you. When you are confident and know your self-worth, it allows you to admire others. It's not that you will never make comparisons or feel badly about yourself at times; it's just that the overall frame should be one of positivity. You can feel great about yourself *and* great about others; you can do both.

Being positive and optimistic is a good thing, and it comes down to making a positive shift in your thinking. Happiness is happiness, whether it comes from what you were able to achieve or accomplish, or from admiring someone else and feeling proud of what they were able to achieve or accomplish. The emotion is the same, regardless of its source. There is this great quote I read long ago from the Dalai Lama: "It's only logical. If I am only happy for myself, many fewer chances for happiness. If I am happy when good things happen to other people, billions more chances to be happy!"

How You Appear to Others

Let's go back to the second aspect of concerns about appearance: how you come across in general. Again, beyond the pressure to look good in photos and social media is the pressure to project an image of competence. Many perfectionists like to look like they have it all together, like they are prepared and ready, and like they are doing it all with ease. This image can become part of one's identity. Yet, most of us feel better and more relaxed around others who don't have it all together; there is a humanness that comes with admitting and accepting flaws. When someone tells you that it took a lot of work, they stayed up late working on it and are now exhausted today, it's real. And when someone is real, they become easy to relate to. We'll talk more about this in Chapter 9.

Remember that others may also be making it look easier than it is. When they act like they didn't study much and still got a "A," didn't practice much and still nailed the audition, look amazing but say they didn't try very hard, they are also projecting an image of having it all together and that their success is seamless and natural (when in reality, a lot of work, effort, and planning went into getting these results).

People-Pleasers

Another perfectionistic behavior that is often motivated by wanting to project a certain image and wanting others to like you is called "people-pleasing." This is when you are accommodating to others, let them lead the way and get what they want, and cater to their needs, rather than asserting your own. People-pleasers find it hard to say "no" for fear of disappointing others, having others be mad at them, or having to deal with a confrontation. They want to be viewed by others in a positive light, and are willing to put their needs second in order to achieve this. Does this describe you? Do you cater to the needs of others to get their approval? If so, make sure to pay attention to the section on people-pleasing in Chapter 8 when you will work on challenging perfectionistic behaviors. The goal here is going to be to learn how to say "no," be assertive, and express your preferences.

A Healthy Relationship With Social Media

The goal here is *not* to not have social media. The goal is to create a balanced relationship with social media. This means you:

1. Manage the amount of time you spend each day on social media.

2. Balance what you look at: don't make it all about friends and acquaintances, look at pages about your interests and hobbies (sports, art, food, health and wellness, fashion, etc.).

3. Take social media breaks.

4. Realize that what you are looking at is constructed and not the whole picture. People are putting out an image they want to project.

5. Be okay with posting the truth. When you are real and authentic or show some vulnerability, it makes you more human

and other people will admire and respect you for it.

6. Do not exaggerate or create your own image of how you'd like to be. For example, post a less flattering picture where you look genuinely excited or happy but maybe your body or clothes aren't a "10."

7. Don't put too much stock in the number of likes or comments you get. Focus more on how much you like what you posted, or how much you like others' posts.

8. Make some of your time an opportunity to spread positivity and make others feel good (when you make a comment, make it heartfelt, give compliments, celebrate others and be happy for their successes).

9. Challenge the tendency to be "all-or-nothing." Instead of making categories like best looking, smartest, winner and loser, describe things in a more neutral or balanced way, without comparisons. For example, give compliments like "impressive—you did a great job" or "great skills."

10. Finally, really consider if going on social media (and which platforms) makes you happy. If it is a source of stress or unhappiness, or makes you feel badly about yourself or an aspect of your life, consider that you have a choice to not be on social media.

Chapter 3
In A Nutshell:

- Social media is constructed and most people only post positive and flattering images of themselves.

- Social media leads to social comparisons, and it's easy to think that others have a better social life and are having more fun than you.

- Perfectionism can also be about appearing to have it all together, making things look easy even though they may have taken a lot of effort.

- Social media isn't bad, but it's important to find a healthy balance!

Chapter 4

A Perfect Body

"

"Beauty lies in the flaws.
Embrace who you are, and
never stop loving yourself."

-Lindsey Vonn, Olympic Skier

"

Everyone can have body image concerns; in fact, when it comes to the eating disorder anorexia, 25% of the cases of young people are male. In general, girls experience pressure to be thin, have flat abs, toned arms and legs, and flawless skin. Plus all the pressures to dress a certain way, be able to style hair, and do makeup...the list goes on! Boys experience a similar pressure to look a certain way. In *Decoding Boys*, the author Dr. Cara Natterson addresses this: "Six-pack abs, no hair on the chest, a full head of hair on the head (or perfectly round, shaved scalp), not a pimple in sight, straight glimmering teeth, broad shoulders, visible biceps, lean but definitely not too thin... The number of items on their unrealistic standards tally goes on."

While exercising and being fit, eating healthy foods, wearing clothing you feel good about, and liking how your hair looks is part of taking good care of yourself and having self-confidence, when perfectionism comes in, these areas of your life can become a larger focus than is reasonable. The joy and creativity are replaced by obsessiveness, with excessive amounts of time spent planning, learning, practicing, doing and re-doing...and then being harshly critical of the results, and pretty much never getting to the point of being satisfied! Lots of people, and often especially teens, eat dangerously in an attempt to look a certain way (whether that's essentially starving themselves to try to lose weight, eating a dangerously high-protein diet in an attempt to gain muscle, or any number of other things).

When it comes to understanding how to improve body image, you have to know what a healthy body image is, which includes how to think about food and exercise. There is hope! There is a positive way to think about your body, eating, and exercise. When your focus becomes about health and well-being (and not the number on the scale), things start to look different. When you learn how to challenge perfectionism and become balanced in these areas, it offers another form of freedom.

The Joy of Eating

Just moments after a baby is born, they are eager to eat. Of course, it's breast milk or formula, but the desire to consume nutrients is a primary instinct. Eating is about nourishing our bodies; it's about health. It's also a source of energy, pleasure, and plays a big role in socializing. When eating becomes more about how you look or how much you weigh, then you have gotten off track in your relationship with food. When you think about food in terms of calories and fat, you are

Take a moment to write down your thoughts about your body:
What do you like, love, or admire about your appearance? It can be a certain feature (like your eyes, the shape of your face, strong muscles, smooth skin) or it can be something broader that relates to your appearance (such as how well you take care of your body, your fashion sense, skin care, or hair styling skills). Whatever you write here should be positive and kind, with no "buts" or qualifiers that discount the positive!

missing out on a true connection with the healthy and nourishing principles of eating. When you are constantly comparing your body to others', you are missing out on the opportunity to feel close to them and the fun of being around them.

So, what does it mean to have a healthy relationship with food and your body? With food, I recommend a balanced approach, such as adapting a version of the 80/20 rule (which we will discuss in more detail in Chapter 7). 80% of the time, eat foods with high nutrients that support the health of your body: things like vegetables, fruits, beans, nuts, fish, whole grains, and olive oil (these are the main components of the Mediterranean diet, which leads to good health in childhood and the teen years, and also promotes longevity). If eating meat, try to make it good quality, like grass-fed beef or organic, free-range chicken. And limit sugar and sugary drinks. Then 20% of the time, chill out a bit and give yourself some flexibility to eat foods that may not be considered all that "clean." If you create a balance in this way, where most of the time (about 80%) you are eating healthfully and a smaller portion of time (20%) you are eating more like people around you are probably eating, then you have nothing to worry about.

There is no need to categorize food as "good" or "bad"—all foods are okay and you can eat all foods. It's just that you create balance between eating a variety of the most nutrient-rich foods with ones with fewer or little nutrients. There is also very little value in thinking about foods in terms of calories or fat grams. From your body's perspective, a calorie from olive oil is not the same as a calorie from a cupcake.

Also, when you think of foods in terms of calories, you are losing your connection with that food. If you eat an apple and think about how few calories it is, then you are not savoring the deliciousness of the apple or focusing on how good it feels to eat an apple. If you eat a brownie and think about how many calories it is, you will feel bad and not savor the deliciousness of the brownie or focus on how fun it feels to eat one. Keep the balance in check, and you will be free from these categories and distracting thoughts. Keep the balance in check, and you will not only enjoy everything you eat, but you will have less to think about and ruminate on when it comes to food.

Food and eating are a big part of socializing. Going to restaurants, picking up food, eating food at parties and gatherings, and making food with friends and romantic partners are all examples of the social aspects of food. When you become perfectionistic about eating, it can interfere with your ability to enjoy eating with others. When you are with friends or at a party, if you don't eat, you are not participating with everyone else. It doesn't mean you need to overeat or overdo it, but you want to give yourself permission to enjoy food with others and make it a habit to eat socially.

A lot of times, perfectionism makes you feel like you are "not allowed" to do things. All-or-nothing thinking and should statements are thinking errors (which we will go over in detail in Chapter 6). All-or-nothing thinking puts food in categories of "good" and "bad" or "allowed" and "not allowed" and puts your weight in categories like "skinny" and "fat." "Should" statements can create rules around eating, like:

- I should eat all clean foods during the week and should only eat treats on the weekends.
- Treats are only allowed if I've exercised that day.
- I should burn as many calories as the treat I ate.
- I will not eat all day so I can eat whatever I want with friends at night.
- I will chew my food for a long time, and eat very, very slowly.
- If I gain a few pounds, I feel like I'm obese.
- To be popular, I have to be skinny.
- People will only be romantically interested in me if I'm fit and have a perfect body.

Also, all-or-nothing thinking can make you feel like you are a "failure" if you ate unhealthy or fattening foods that day. It can also be that you were "perfect" all day with your eating and then ate something "bad" at night, resulting in feeling like you "ruined" a "perfect" day of eating. Not only are these categorizations unnatural, they don't offer any flexibility. The key is to be flexible and allow yourself to be balanced in the way you eat, avoid judging yourself, and definitely don't shame or blame yourself for something you ate!

Perfectionism involves a drive for control. Sometimes this sense of control gets played out with eating and dieting. Deciding in advance what you will eat and how much you will eat is a form of control, and again, is not a natural approach to eating. We need to eat until we feel satisfied and stop when we do. Weighing yourself every day is another form of perfectionistic control. I recommend getting rid of the scale if you are doing this. I also have a joke about scales: if you weigh yourself, you will eat cookies. If you weigh yourself and you weigh less than you were expecting, now you can have a cookie. But if you weigh yourself and weigh more than you were expecting... well, since you weigh too much anyway, you might as well have a cookie. Either way, you end up eating a cookie! It's

Take a moment to think or write about your relationship with food:

- When you think about eating, do you label your food in terms of categories? Do you feel bad after you eat certain foods? Write about any judgments you make about yourself when eating.

- How would you like to think about food and eating? What thoughts would support a more positive experience for you when eating?

better to not weigh yourself and instead focus on how you feel in your body.

Exercise Obsession

Exercise can also be taken over by perfectionism, making it an obsession and making your self-worth about how much and how effectively you have exercised. Our bodies are designed to move, but again, there needs to be balance to this. When you calculate your workouts, measuring your sets, calories burned, not stopping until exactly 60 minutes or six miles precisely, and so on, and the focus becomes on these calculations, you miss the benefits (especially the mental ones) of exercise. You miss the feeling of happiness and release that comes with exercising.

There are certain competitive sports that promote weight-loss, staying within a certain weight range, or mastering a certain body type.

For example, wrestling, gymnastics, rowing, dance, ballet, skating, and swimming can all foster an unhealthy drive to reach a certain weight or maintain a certain physique. This doesn't mean these sports are bad, but they may not be the best choice for everyone. If you participate in these sports and find yourself having an imbalanced relationship with food and exercise or an obsession with looking a certain way for your sport, it's time to consider if it's worth it. Perfectionism can make it hard to let things go, to be able to be flexible and to reconsider your participation in something you've committed to. But sometimes it's important to.

If your sport is impacting your health or your self-esteem negatively, have a conversation with your parent and your coach to see what can be done to help you gain more balance. How much of it is you and how much of it is the sport? Sometimes it's coming from the coach or parental pressure. Try to problem-solve and personally challenge yourself before figuring out if you can keep doing it or not. If you end up deciding that the sport itself is providing too much pressure, give yourself permission to find a different activity or interest to invest in.

Find a Balance

Health comes first when it comes to food and eating, and being balanced about how you eat will make it more likely that you can maintain overall healthy eating in the long-term. A lot of people try to diet to lose weight, but we know diets are ineffective and do not lead to sustainable weight loss. The diet industry (including books on diets) is a billion-dollar industry, yet it won't give you the answers when it comes down to knowing how to eat in a balanced, healthy way. Dieting also puts you at risk for developing an eating disorder. When you eat in a balanced way, exercise for your physical and mental health, and sleep enough, you will be at your best. Learning how to treat your body well is part of having a good body image.

My goal is for you to love yourself and love your body. Perfectionism commonly interferes with both: it makes you critical of yourself and whatever you do, and makes you critical of how you look. Perfectionism holds the ideal body as the goal. Yet, most people don't have the body of a model, six-pack abs, or perfectly clear skin. While any of this *may* be attainable, the cost of doing so is often very high. For a healthy body image, the goal is body confidence, not perfection. The goal is to love your looks, be grateful for your health, and be grateful for what your body can do. Having a healthy body image means you are not critically judging your shape and focusing on what you want to look different. Some people with perfectionism feel so much shame about their bodies and appearance that they avoid social activities or (if age appropriate) being physical with others. They avoid dating or pursuing romantic interests. They avoid being around others and putting themselves out there because of how they look. They may wear clothes that are too big in order to hide their body. If this describes you, you need to focus on the self-kindness part of self-compassion: why don't you get to be social and enjoy life? You deserve the same as everyone else. You will also notice that when others feel good about themselves and project confidence, they have good energy and others want to be around them. Being a confident person and feeling good about yourself, including how you look, draws others to you. When you think it's about appearance, you are neglecting to see the bigger picture of what makes someone attractive.

What do you already love about your appearance? What is your best asset? What do you wish were different, and how can you challenge yourself to accept yourself as you are? Do you have a flabby stomach or a face that tends to break out?

Can you love yourself and give yourself permission to live life fully, without needing these things to change? Can you allow yourself to wear the clothes you like? How does focusing on the parts you don't like benefit you? It probably doesn't help much!

Many times, when you change your perfectionistic behaviors around eating and exercising, stop comparisons with others on how they look (and remember that social media images are not reality), and replace shaming inner self-talk with self-kindness and self-love, your body image will improve. When you look at yourself and notice what is *right* and focus on what you like about what you see, you will feel better about your appearance and feel better in general, which will make others feel drawn to you. There is no doubt that cultivating a positive body image and prioritizing your health and well-being will have a big pay-off.

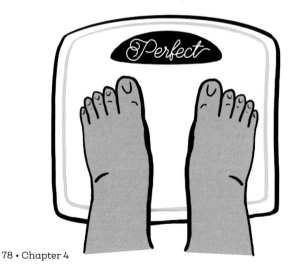

Chapter 4
In A Nutshell:

- A heightened focus on body image can make it hard to feel good about how you look and can become a time-consuming preoccupation.

- Perfectionism can make eating a challenge, making food all about calories and rules. Focus on a balance, like the 80/20 rule, instead!

- Perfectionism can make something natural like exercising and moving your body into a controlled, negative experience. Try to focus on exercise and movement that makes you feel good, physically and emotionally.

Chapter 5

Cognitive-Behavioral Therapy for Perfectionism

"

"The secret to change is to
focus all of your energy, not
on fighting the old, but on
building the new."

-Socrates

"

So now we've talked all about what perfectionism is, how it impacts life, and some ways to
cope with it. But how can we actually *change* it?

Cognitive-behavioral therapy (CBT) is a type of
therapy that is about learning strategies to change
your thoughts and behavior. Much of the focus is on
one's thoughts and thinking patterns. CBT has been
proven to be an effective way to treat perfectionism.
It is also the most supported approach to treating
anxiety and depression. CBT is structured, offers
solutions, and is results-oriented. It's also usually
a short-term process, unlike some other therapies
that can last for years.

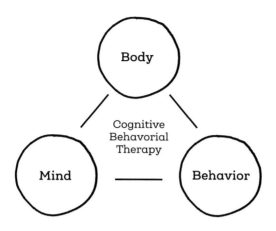

Cognitive
Behavorial
Therapy

Body

Mind

Behavior

When we look at perfectionism and the related stress or anxiety that often accompanies it, CBT focuses on addressing three aspects: symptoms that show up in the body (physical feelings and emotions), mind (thoughts), and behavior (actions). For example, when preparing for a big assignment, your body can be tense and you might even have stomachaches or headaches, your thoughts are about needing the grade to be a "perfect A," and your actions are to send multiple emails with many specific questions to the teacher, spend many more hours than needed to get it done, or procrastinate. Sometimes, perfectionists do not have many body symptoms, and its mostly perfectionistic thoughts and behaviors. This chapter will provide an overview of what CBT is and how it is used to address perfectionism. The chapters that follow will go into more detail about the three parts.

Body

Cognitive-behavioral therapy involves learning ways to relax the body. This can involve calm breathing, mindfulness training, meditation, yoga, and guided imagery or visualization. When your perfectionism causes stress, that stress can come up in the body, either as physical symptoms or as a general feeling of restlessness. Even if you don't have any physiological symptoms of perfectionism or stress, it's always good to learn relaxation techniques, as they help relax the mind as well. Chapter 10 will focus on this and self-care in general, and will include some good apps that other teens have enjoyed and found helpful.

Take a moment to consider or write down how perfectionism shows up in your body. How does your body feel when you are in the throes of perfectionistic thoughts and behaviors? Can you think of a time when you felt completely relaxed and light in your body? How does your body change from being calm to being worried about being perfect? For example, do you have muscle tension or get stomachaches or headaches? Do you notice times of exhaustion or fatigue? Does this ever come up when you are over-preparing for something?

Mind

CBT also involves the use of strategies and techniques focused on changing one's thoughts. Our thoughts impact how we behave. For example, if you think it's only worth being on the basketball team if you are guaranteed to be a starter, then you won't move forward and join the team if you are told you'd be a back-up. It's similar to mindset: if you have a fixed mindset and believe you are either naturally good at doing something or not, you will give up after a few unsuccessful tries. Your behavior is a result of your thinking process.

When you work at changing your thoughts, this is called "cognitive restructuring." For example, let's say you're scared to drive on the highway because you think it is more dangerous. Then you learn about the statistics showing that the majority of driving fatalities are on rural roads and not highways; you should then be less nervous about driving on highways. So, changing the way you think about it will change the way you feel about it, and you will be more likely to not only drive on the highway, but be less worried when doing so. It all comes down to the thoughts you choose to focus on. When you've been in the habit of perfectionistic thinking, it can be challenging to see your thoughts for what they are; it's hard to even recognize that your way of thinking is something that should be changed.

We'll learn to challenge perfectionistic thoughts by examining your core beliefs (the main beliefs you have about yourself, others, and the world), breaking the rumination cycle (that tendency to obsess over a single thing you or someone else said or did), challenging thinking errors, and practicing compassionate self-talk.

This is a good time to take a moment and write down three perfectionistic thoughts or beliefs. For example, do you think things fall into two categories: either perfect or failure? Do you look at others and compare how your body measures up to theirs? Do you believe only an "A+" is good enough? Do you go over a little mistake in your head repeatedly, feeling more and more guilty and upset the longer you think about it? Do you believe it's not worth doing something unless you can be #1? Do you worry about disappointing others if you don't perform your best? What do you think about others when they make a mistake?

Behavior

The main goal of CBT when it comes to behavior, is to challenge avoidance or other actions that are done in the service of perfectionism. Asking for reassurance, having trouble delegating tasks to others, re-doing something over and over, and avoiding taking risky shots in your sport are examples of perfectionistic actions to challenge. With CBT, the principle is: you must face your fears to overcome them. If you don't challenge your own actions, the fears underlying the perfectionism will not go away. By purposely challenging your perfectionism and doing practices of things you would usually avoid, you will learn that it's not as bad as you had expected. By going outside of your comfort zone, you will learn to be able to tolerate the discomfort that comes from things not working out as you had expected. Over time, by repeating the practices, you will *habituate*, or become used to doing things differently.

An interesting note about CBT:

Your behavior change will happen first and then your thoughts will change.

For example, let's say you will challenge your perfectionism and really push yourself outside your comfort zone by earning a "B" on an assignment on purpose: that is a behavior change. You make this behavior change first, before you will be able to think that getting a "B" is okay (which is a thought change). It's like you have to step outside of your comfort zone before you can see that nothing bad will happen from doing so.

Here's an example: Kelly, who was well-liked by others, was encouraged to work on her perfectionism by her parents because they wanted her to "have more fun" and "chill out" rather than spending seven days a week studying hard and doing work. When it was first suggested that she try getting a B on a math assignment, she was horrified and asked: "Why would you want me to fail?" I asked if she felt getting a "B" was failing. We discussed how she needed to have a sample of what she experienced as failure in order to make sure she could deal with it. Eventually, she agreed and got a 'B' on her homework (while happily maintaining her A in the class; math was her favorite subject) and realized that nothing bad happened. She realized she could handle it. At the same time, she made an effort to have one social plan over the weekend and one social plan during one of the weekdays after school, building up to three or four social plans a week. She also challenged herself to have one weekend day each week where she didn't do any homework or study. Over the course of several months, she not only saw her grades stay the same, but she watched her friendships get stronger, and her sense of self grow. She was more confident, more relaxed, and reported feeling happier. One of those social plans each week involved doing a spin class with her friend, and she discovered how much she enjoyed exercising. In addition (and this was not really the goal, but it's not a bad thing), she reported that she was more efficient at getting her schoolwork done. She explained that when she felt she had the whole weekend to work, she would drag it out and make it last the whole weekend! I told her this reminded me of when I pack for a trip: if I take a large suitcase, even for just a three-night trip, I will end up filling it. She was getting her work done faster and told me she felt this was good preparation for high school, when she would undoubtedly have more work to do.

None of these good results started with a change in her thinking; rather, it was the result of changing her behavior. Most people never regret stepping outside of their comfort zone, and neither did she! Even if her grades had changed a bit, the gains she made from challenging her perfectionism and learning how to work more efficiently, and the freedom she experienced from doing so, far outweighed the potential loss of a lowered grade.

In the next few chapters, we'll use CBT to help challenge your perfectionism. When it comes to changing behaviors and venturing outside of your comfort zone, you will be the one to set the pace.

Chapter 5 In A Nutshell:

- Cognitive-behavioral therapy works on changing established patterns in your body, mind, and behavior.

- Perfectionism can make you stressed, which can come up in your body, so learning how to calm the body is key.

- Thinking errors, core beliefs, rumination, negative self-talk, and avoidance behaviors all play a role in perfectionism.

- Behavior changes come before thinking changes!

Chapter 6

Challenging Perfectionistic Thinking

66

"Change your thoughts and you change your world."

-Norman Vincent Peale, author of The Power of Positive Thinking

"The greatest discovery of my generation is that human beings can alter their lives by altering their attitudes of mind."

-William James, considered the "Father of American Psychology"

99

This is perhaps one of the most important chapters of this book. This is where most perfectionists really need to work hard to change, but the payoff can also be the greatest. Changing one's thoughts and one's perspective is no easy accomplishment, but it can be done, and can make an enormous difference.

There are four key components that we have to address in order to tackle perfectionist thinking:

- Thinking errors (also called cognitive distortions)
- Core beliefs
- The cycle of worrying and ruminating
- Self-talk

Changing your perspective and coming up with a new thinking pattern so you can see a situation in a different way is called cognitive restructuring. The main goal of changing how you think is to feel better and have a more positive outlook on life. When a situation comes up, your automatic thoughts color it for you; we tend to have the same thoughts and make the same interpretations over and over. It becomes a habit to think this way. But habits can be broken, and we can develop new ones. You can change your way of thinking, because you are in charge of your thoughts.

Thinking Errors

In order to develop new thinking patterns, you first need to identify which thinking errors you tend to make. Thinking errors are also called "cognitive distortions." Everyone makes thinking errors, and perfectionists tend to make certain ones more than others. Regardless of which ones you make, the goal is to figure out when you are making them and come up with a different pattern of thinking. For example, I used to be an all-or-nothing thinker and would think in extremes—things were either exactly how I wanted them to be or I didn't like them at all. If something I bought had a scratch on it (literally), I felt like it was ruined. Same for a book with bent pages. If plans changed last minute, or were cancelled, it felt like the whole day was messed up, and even though I'd move through the day, I kept focusing on the original plan that never happened. I liked to follow the rules and perhaps was a bit rigid at times. My friends in high school would jokingly (but lovingly) call me "R&R" (which stood for Rules & Regulations!) because I would be the one to make sure we would be home before a curfew and did things responsibly...but sometimes at the expense of being relaxed and truly in the moment. In college and graduate school, I began to chill out a bit but still had all-or-nothing thoughts. I eventually challenged this pattern in my late 20s, as I became a psychologist and realized that it was a barrier to becoming my best self. I had to learn how to be flexible in my thinking and flexible in general. To do this, I would often cue myself with the following self-talk: *What would someone who is flexible think in this situation? What would they do?* And then, after challenging myself over and over when dealing with changes, I was able to see that things ended up working out even if they were different than I expected them to be. I purposely practiced letting others make the plans and just went with it. I made myself keep things that were scratched and books that arrived with bent corners.

I learned to be okay with these imperfections and still love the objects just the same. I became more flexible with the daily goals I set for myself, sometimes letting them go to do something spontaneous and fun. I no longer had all-or-nothing thinking as an automatic thought. By my early 30s, I had become a quite flexible person. I am hoping to save you from waiting that long to make this positive change!

All-or-Nothing Thinking

This is also called "black-and-white thinking," and it's when you see things in two extreme categories: perfect or a failure. There is no in-between; it's either exactly as you want it to be or it's terrible. All-or-nothing thinking usually involves having rigid expectations, and the bar gets set extremely high, because you want it to be perfect. The consequences of thinking this way are real, and often involve feeling disappointment in yourself or others; for example, if you are only satisfied with an "A+" and earning anything less than 100% on a test feels like failing, when you get a 97%, all of your focus is on what you could have done to get the extra 3%. Instead of feeling good about your "A" and celebrating yourself, you feel inadequate and it may even become a sign for you that you don't measure up. Or if your friend cancels plans on you last minute, you may think that you don't want to be friends with someone who cancels on you. There is little room for making errors or mistakes or being flexible. I've known children and teens who accidentally drew a mark on their artwork and wanted to get rid of it; others who gained a few pounds and labeled themselves as "fat," concluding that nobody will like them with the extra pounds; and others who couldn't look past a mistake, labeling themselves as "stupid" and "a complete failure," or replaying over and over the correction a teacher made on their work, feeling terrible about themselves for not getting it right the first time. You may plan to try out for a team and then, because you fear your skills won't be good enough to make it, decide to pull out of the try-outs.

Once you are aware of your tendency to think this way, the goal is to notice your thinking as it arises when you are in the situation. Then cue yourself: *I can try to be flexible here. What would someone who is flexible do? In the end, it won't matter if I do it differently, but it will help to learn a new way of thinking. I can do this.* Work with yourself to notice the automatic thought and then replace it with a more balanced one. The other option, as we will discuss later, is to come up with a few practices you can do to purposely challenge all-or-nothing thinking; for example, picking out an imperfect thing to buy, like damaged fruit or a used or bent book, asking your parent or friend to switch up the plans last minute so you can practice handling it, doing something you're not good at, or purposely making a mistake on a graded assignment. These kinds of behavioral challenges will give you the experience you need to see that you can be fine when things are not as you expected or wanted them to be. You will learn that it ends up working out okay.

Filtering

This is when you focus on the bad and ignore the good. You think about what went wrong instead of what went right. This type of negative thinking makes you feel unhappy. For example, let's say you had a birthday party and invited ten close friends for a sleepover. All ten said they would be there, but then on the day of the party, one friend texted that they couldn't come because they felt sick and another friend let you know they were planning to come but not sleep over. The next day, when your parents asked how the party was, you focus only on the friend who was too sick to come and the other one who left early. All of the fun of the party becomes overshadowed by the two that didn't fully participate. The same is true when you ruminate on the shot you missed in soccer instead of focusing on the multiple times you assisted your team in making a goal, or the many parts of your appearance and body that you do like but barely notice because you're always staring at the one or two things you don't like.

To challenge filtering, we want to focus more on the positive and what went well, and learn to think in a positive, healthy way. This also relates to gratitude, and while we will look into this in more depth in Chapter 11, it's worth mentioning that when you are thinking of what went well and what you are grateful for (having gratitude), you are then not focused on what did not go well or what is missing (feeling deprived). Gratitude is the opposite of deprivation. When you challenge the filtering thinking error and adopt a gratitude mindset, you will find yourself in a happier state with more energy for life.

To do this, go into a situation and make the goal to identify five things that went well. Notice what there is to be grateful about. What makes you lucky in this situation, or what do you have going for you? Even if it's not a positive situation, what are you learning by being there, and how will those lessons benefit you? By being intentional about it, you can learn to shift your focus and change your perspective.

Catastrophizing

This is also called "What if" thinking, and it's when you think the worst is going to happen, or you exaggerate how bad something is. "If I fail this test, I won't get into college" is a perfect example of catastrophizing. Another example is "What if I don't get into the photography club? Then there's no way I will become a real photographer." These thoughts easily trigger feeling worked up and even panicky. When you turn up the importance of an obstacle, making it feel unmanageable, you undermine your ability to problem-solve and be resilient. Most of the time, these perceived catastrophes end up being no big deal and we work through them. Logically, you might think that the next time you had this situation you wouldn't worry as much, but the opposite happens: the worry and panic become associated with a good outcome. Instead of realizing there was nothing to really worry about, the worry cycle gets reinforced!

The goal with catastrophizing is to recognize when you are doing it. Labeling it can help to minimize it: *Oh, there I go again, catastrophizing as usual. How would someone who is confident and resilient think in this situation?* Most of the time, just knowing you have a tendency to catastrophize can help you recognize and shift it. It can also help to think of the most likely outcome, or trust that things will just work out and be okay. It might sound like: *If I don't get into the photography club, it will be disappointing, but that won't change how invested I am in my photography. I can't force them to let me in, so it's outside of my control. But what I do with my photography is within my control.*

Finally, you want to have a "resilient mindset" and know you can handle whatever comes your way. Try some of the compassionate self-talk we discussed in Chapter 2. Have a confident attitude and believe in your ability to problem-solve and handle whatever happens.

Shoulds

"Shoulds" are rules you have made up about how you expect or believe things should be. When it comes to perfectionism, this could sound like *I should get on the varsity team, I should excel at everything I put effort into, I should be included when my two friends get together,* and *I shouldn't make mistakes.* The problem with making "shoulds" as rules in your life is that things don't always work out how we'd like them to, and people don't always respond the way we want them to; there is no flexibility in should statements. It sets you up to be disappointed in yourself and in others.

Challenge yourself to not live by these self-imposed rules. If you made these rules, you can change them. Usually, shoulds are another way of being harsh and critical with yourself or others; recognize that not everyone makes should-statements, and you don't need to either. Acknowledge that there are so many ways of doing things; everyone thinks and operates differently, and that's okay. People operate from their own perspective and won't always see a situation the way you do. In his book *You Can Be Happy No Matter What*, Dr. Richard Carlson talks about being right versus being happy, and how if your goal is to prove you are right, you will miss out on being happy and connected in your relationships. Most people don't intend to wrong you, and most people cannot read your mind or anticipate what you want from them. Relaxing these rules will give you more flexibility to feel more connected to others and to focus more on what really matters. If you observe yourself going into "shoulds" mode, challenge it by asking yourself: *What would someone who is flexible think in this situation? How do I handle this with compassion and understanding? If it's a should rule, it's coming from a place of perfectionism and I can challenge it.*

Personalization

Personalization is when you think things, particularly negative events, are about you, even though in reality they are completely unrelated to you. The majority of perfectionists like to follow the rules and not get in trouble. Perhaps a teacher makes a general announcement to the class that the honor code must be followed precisely, or students will get in trouble. That general message could get personalized by a perfectionist student, meaning that they think the message was for them specifically! Personalization can also be when you take responsibility for a negative outcome when it really has nothing to do with you. For example, someone might look at you and you think they are judging you or what you are wearing. In reality, it could be that they are admiring what you are wearing, or not thinking anything about you but just happened to look in your direction. Another example could be if you chose a movie for you and your friends that turned out to be pretty bad. You leave feeling embarrassed and, in your mind, feel responsible for the bad movie (as if you were the director of it!). Personalization is also at the root of feeling badly or inadequate when someone else achieves or accomplishes something (it overlaps with social comparisons there). For example, if your teacher compliments someone else's work, but not yours, and you interpret this to mean that they didn't like your work. You may end up feeling criticized when there was actually no criticism, since your teacher's compliment to someone else has nothing to do with how they feel about your work.

Once you become better at identifying when you are personalizing, it will be easier to shift your thinking by asking yourself: *What's another way of thinking about this? What is a way of seeing this situation that has nothing to do with me?* Like most of these thinking traps, just learning to recognize when you're doing it can have a huge impact on reducing it.

Mind-Reading

This thinking error is when you think you know what others are thinking or saying about you. It's a bit similar to personalization in that you are taking personally things that may actually have nothing to do with you. Often, the assumption here is negative: that others are thinking badly about you. For example, your teacher who directs the school play gave you the fourth leading role, even though you tried out for the lead, and you think he must not really like you and thinks you didn't really try hard enough at the auditions. Another example could be that you gave a birthday present to your friend and he said "thanks so much," and you think he must not have liked it that much—because you think if he really loved it, he would have had more to say. Or if your aunt comes over and comments how big you've gotten, and you interpret this as meaning she thinks you are fat. And on and on. Since perfectionism makes you a harsh critic of yourself, when you are mind-reading, you will likely project that others are judging you in the same fashion. In reality, people are far more kind and forgiving of others than they are of themselves.

I once talked to a teenager who told me none of his friend's parents liked him; as we discussed it further, it was clear that he was mind-reading and made up all these reasons why, explaining "I think this parent sees me as too much work to have over," and "this other dad never really asks me much when he sees me." Most of the explanations were random and without any real evidence. This is how mind-reading works: the thoughts are being generated by you and are only your view of what others are thinking. With mind-reading, it's really useful to examine the evidence and look for proof that your thought is either right or wrong. What support is there for that conclusion, and what evidence can you find that discounts what you believe to be true? While it's true that not everyone will like us, for the most part, without any real words or behavior that clearly expresses a negative emotion from another, the assumption should be that people will view you favorably.

Selective Attention

Selective attention is when you pay attention to information that confirms your beliefs and ignore information that goes against or discredits them. For example, if you think you need to be really thin and in shape to be liked by others, you will only notice your most popular peers who happen to be really thin and fit and use that as evidence to support your belief. You will ignore other evidence that goes against this belief. You won't focus on the peers who have more average shapes and are equally as popular and well-liked. Or, let's say you give a presentation to your class and, while many of the other students are actively interested, there are two or three kids who are not (they're looking around the room, about to fall sleep, or doodling on their notebook); at the end of the presentation, you focus on the three who weren't very engaged, and you conclude that your presentation was not very interesting or you are not a good presenter.

When it comes to your beliefs, try seeing what evidence there is that supports the opposite; be a good researcher about it—don't just look for the evidence you want to find. You can even do a little experiment on selective attention: pick a random opinion and then search the internet to support it. For example, search "alien abductions are real" and you will find "evidence" to support that; but of course if you search "alien abductions faked," you'll find evidence for them all being hoaxes! If you never look for opposing evidence, it's easy to think one belief is true. The news is a great example of selective attention. If you believe the world is a dangerous place, just turn on the news and you will hear about all the terrible and scary things going on in the world. But the news ignores all the times that nothing happens; there aren't reports on peaceful, uneventful days!

Cognitive Shifts for Each Thinking Error

Thinking Error	Replace with:
All-or-Nothing Thinking	Flexibility
Filtering	Focus on the positive & what went well Cultivate gratitude
Catastrophizing	Label the error Resilience/Confidence Realize you can handle it
Shoulds	Flexibility
Personalization	See that there are many explanations for the same event
Mind-Reading	Alternative explanations that aren't about you
Selective Attention	Look for evidence to support alternative beliefs

Create a Thoughts Log

To challenge automatic thoughts and thinking errors, you can create a "thoughts log," which involves recording your automatic thoughts and coming up with new, replacement thoughts. Doing this in a structured, consistent way, like in a notebook or on your phone, will also help you keep track of progress.

Here is an example of how to track and challenge your thinking errors:

Situation:

You love math and decide to participate in the mathnasium competition at school. Participants were told that no preparation is needed and it's being held in the spirit of fun and a love for math.

What are your first, automatic thoughts? Can you find any thinking errors?

I have to come in first (all-or-nothing thinking). If I don't win this, then I'm not as good at math as I thought (catastrophizing). And if I don't come in first, my teacher will likely be disappointed (mind reading). I should only do this if I put in 100% so I'm going to spend the whole weekend studying and taking practice tests (shoulds, all-or-nothing).

How do the automatic thought(s) make you feel?

Pressured and stressed, but also excited by the idea of winning it.
   Like I need to impress my teacher and keep up my reputation with her.

How did it turn out? Did your automatic thoughts serve you well?

I came in second place, despite practicing all weekend. Instead of having fun during the competition, I was stressed out the whole time and kept looking over to the other students to see how quickly they were working. This probably slowed me down. My math teacher was there and was so excited and proud of me for coming in 2nd, but I couldn't feel good about it and kept thinking that I must not be as good as I thought and probably shouldn't have done the competition at all.

How would someone without perfectionism think?
What are new, more balanced, more self-compassionate
thoughts about this situation?

It would have been better if I had
been more flexible and had more
self-compassion. I could've thought:
This is supposed to be fun, and they
said that no preparation is needed,
so I'm just going to do it and give
it my all. I'm proud of myself for
participating since I love math, and
my teacher will be proud of me for
taking part in it.

To create your own log, using a notebook or even your phone, make five sections:

- Situation
- Automatic thoughts (label any of them that are thinking errors)
- Feelings
- Outcome
- Replacement thoughts (balanced, self-compassionate thoughts)

If you want to do more in-depth work on challenging your thinking errors and patterns,

I highly recommend, Dr. Mary Alvord's workbook, *Conquer Negative Thinking for Teens*.

Core Beliefs

Core beliefs are beliefs and assumptions you have about yourself, others, and the world. When you are perfectionistic, you tend to have firmly held beliefs about what equals success. Core beliefs are at the root of automatic thoughts. For example, the automatic thought of "What's wrong with me? I'm so stupid!" in response to making a mistake is likely rooted in the core believe if you or others make mistakes, then it means that you are inadequate.

A core belief is like a template, and when new information comes in, you fit it into that template. It can be helpful because it makes you more efficient at interpreting information and drawing conclusions; however, it can also make you too quick to assume or judge without considering all the other factors that play a role. Core beliefs can become strengthened when you use selective attention, as both concepts shape information to fit with your ideas about the world.

It can be hard to change core beliefs, but they *can* be changed. You have to take in information in a fresh way and be open to letting this new interpretation change the way you usually see things. This new set of core beliefs will be more flexible and compassionate. Changing your behavior and learning that you can handle things you previously thought were too difficult, and learning that a new way of doing things turned out okay, also helps challenge the core belief.

As you move forward in challenging your perfectionism, changing your behavior and having new experiences will offer a good opportunity to modify your core beliefs and develop new ones.

Let's go through a quick example. Assume that you think your self-worth is based on excelling in everything you do: how well you do in school, at violin, and in keeping fit. In your mind, when you thrive in all three areas, all is well. The core belief is: *as long as I am performing my best, I am valuable and worthy and can feel good about myself.* But then you come in 3rd place in a violin competition and suddenly you feel like a total failure, like you can't handle anything, like you disappointed your teacher and parents, and should give up violin because why devote so much time and effort to only come in 3rd! The core belief causes you to see only one path to feeling self-worth: performing well in all areas. A better belief would be: *who I am, someone who has many interests and does a lot, is doing great in life. I may not always be perfect, but I'm doing well.* This core belief offers a broader definition of success: it's not all about the exact grades or place in the competition. It's a broader view of *wow, I am someone who does a lot, has a lot of interests and pursuits that I enjoy and take pride in, and is doing a pretty great job in life. I am also a loving person who show kindness towards others.* A belief like this one is protective: it keeps your self-esteem intact and makes sure that how you feel about yourself is not conditionally based on how well you do in certain areas of life.

Worry & Rumination Cycle

When you have perfectionism, you tend to focus on wanting to be the best, performing and achieving well in whatever you do. As a result, you get worries and the tendency to ruminate (when you think about something over and over again). Perfectionism often wants predictability and certainty, but the world is filled with unpredictability and uncertainty. To challenge the worry cycle, we need to learn how to tolerate ambiguity and uncertainty.

When you are perfectionistic, it's very common to get stuck on little errors you make, like something you said to someone that you wish you hadn't said. You might also get stuck on things *other* people do, like a comment someone made to you, a slight correction, or something they said that made you feel like they were upset with you. These little things happen to everyone all the time, and they are not worth honing in on; however, with perfectionism, your radar for these subtle or slight things is very sensitive. Once you pick up on one, it can become a focus area for you, causing you to worry about it, ruminating and wishing you could go back and undo it. The goal here is to recognize that everyone experiences these moments, that you can't go back and change it, and that you have to accept it as nothing that important and move on.

The thoughts log from earlier is a great way to disrupt the rumination cycle. Write down your thoughts, identify and label the thinking errors, and come up with replacement thoughts. For the replacement thoughts, these are new ways of seeing or thinking about the situation, and they reflect what someone without perfectionism would think. We often experience our thoughts as facts and this is a good way to challenge them. Doing this also helps to see your thoughts as an observer.

If you find yourself stuck in a rumination cycle, another very effective strategy is to make a loop recording of your thoughts and listen to it over and over until the brain views the thoughts as neutral or boring. You can make the recording on a phone (voice memos); it should be in your own voice, just what you sound like as you are having these worries, doubts, and concerns. You can write it all out first and then listen to it back, over and over, for about 10 minutes a day. There are two goals in doing a loop recording: to be able to hear yourself and learn to become an *observer* of your ruminating thoughts (rather than a participant in them, which is when you get all caught up in them) and for your brain to become bored so these thoughts will lose their hold on you (which will happen naturally as you hear the same thing over and over!).

The same strategy works for dealing with uncertainty. Write down all of the possible outcomes (what could happen if...) for situations you are worried about. Then change this list into an uncertainty list: "It's possible that I won't become a photographer" or "It's possible that the coach likes my friend better than me." Make a recording of these uncertainty statements and do the same thing as with the worries: listen back over and over until your brain is bored! Once these statements no longer get you upset, then you know the recording has worked. For some, it takes only a few days, but for most, it takes at least two or three weeks (or more!) for the thoughts to lose their power and become boring.

Finally, if you find yourself ruminating or second-guessing yourself at a time when you cannot do one of these strategies, an effective technique is to use distraction to unhook yourself from your thoughts. Making a list in your head, for example, of all 50 states in alphabetical order, or making lists like "five things that are turquoise" or "five things in my backpack" really works. A favorite for people I know is to make a list of things using the alphabet (which I used as distraction from ordering blueberry scones to delay gratification), such as fruits/vegetables: Apple, Banana, Carrot, Date, Eggplant, Fig, Grapes.... Or colleges: Arizona State, Boston College, Colgate, Dartmouth, Emory, Florida State University, George Washington University... When you bring your attention to something else like this, it allows your mind to calm down and detach from whatever was triggering you to feel anxious or worried.

Self-Talk

Self-talk refers to your inner dialogue and the messages you give yourself. Replacing old, negative self-talk with more positive messages is another way to override perfectionism. When you work with the messages you give yourself, you are living your life with more intention, rather than just accepting negativity. We want the messages we give ourselves to be positive, energizing, and to reflect a "can-do" attitude, rather than being critical or negative. Research shows that when you have positive thinking, more neurons develop in the left prefrontal cortex (the "cool," thinking system), making you even better at coping and managing life.

Unsupportive Self-Talk	Supportive Self-Talk
I'll never get this done.	I can do this.
I'm an idiot and have no idea how to do this.	I believe in myself.
This all needs to get done now!	Let me take one step at a time.
What's wrong with me?	It's okay that this is hard for me.
I can't do anything right.	I can handle it!

Do any of these unsupportive statements sound familiar? The inner voice of many perfectionists actually sounds this harsh! Perfectionism can make you feel like you're not doing anything right, and because of all-or-nothing thinking, mistakes are not allowed. But we all make mistakes. And we need them and need to fail in order to learn and become better.

Remember we reviewed the importance of self-compassion and how people who have self-compassion, rather than self-criticism, are better at meeting their goals? And how self-compassion as a concept is very much related to being successful? Well, it's wise then to integrate self-compassion statements into your self-talk, replacing the (likely harsh and demanding) ones you are naturally using with yourself. Remember that self-compassion involves self-kindness, common humanity, and mindfulness. So here are some sample self-talk statements that reflect the spirit of those three principles:

- It's okay that I'm struggling right now.
- It's okay that it didn't turn out how I wanted.
- It's okay that it isn't perfect.
- Everyone makes mistakes.
- Everyone has a rough patch, a bad day, an embarrassing moment. I am human, too!
- I can be disappointed and I can handle it.
- What would I say to my friend right now?
- How would someone with self-kindness think about this?
- I can see how disappointed I feel and that's okay.
- I can see I'm having a hard time dealing with this right now. I know it's just because I care so much.
- I appreciate how hard I worked on this, even if I don't like my grade.
- I'm proud of myself for trying out, even if I didn't' make it.
- It's good that I'm the kind of person who takes risks and puts myself out there.

We also want our self-talk to reflect the other factors that relate to success, including a resilience mindset, growth mindset, grit, an internal locus of control, self-efficacy, delay of gratification, and creativity. And of course, we want to use self-talk statements that inspire self-confidence. Self-talk focusing on those principles might sound like:

- I can handle whatever comes my way.
- I'm uncomfortable and I can handle this.
- Every problem has a solution.
- I will not give up. I will stick with it.
- I believe in myself. I can do this.
- What can I change in this situation? How can I think about this differently?
- How would someone who is flexible think in this situation?
- Others will make mistakes. I can be patient and not react.
- There is a lot I can do to impact this situation.
- Who can I ask for help?
- What else can I try doing?
- If others can stick with it, so can I. By staying with it, I will figure it out.
- Things should not always come easily. It's okay to not be a natural at something and keep working at it.
- Just because I set the bar so high doesn't mean I failed. Someone who didn't set it so high would be more aware of how well they did.
- I know there's another way of seeing this.
- I know I can get this done.
- I don't need to get this whole list done right now. I can do it over a few days. It doesn't have to be completed all at once.

I recommend that you take a bunch of notecards and write some of these statements on them, picking the ones that would be most helpful to you. You can read them over and over and identify a few that you really connect with to memorize. Also, try to come up with some of your own that specifically relate to areas your perfectionism impacts. For example, you might make self-talk cards that focus on tennis, lacrosse, dance, piano, body image, or friendships and expectations of others.

Chapter 6
In A Nutshell:

- Perfectionism often shows up as thinking errors such as all-or-nothing thinking, filtering, catastrophizing, personalization, mind-reading, should statements, and selective attention.

- The goal is to replace thinking errors with balanced thoughts and learning how to see situations differently.

- We all have core beliefs about ourselves, others, and the world. Sometimes we have to challenge these core beliefs in order to live a more fulfilling life.

- Thought logs, loop recordings, and distraction can all be used to break the rumination cycle.

- The goal is to have positive, supportive self-talk such as, "Every problem has a solution" and "I know there is another way of seeing this."

Chapter 7

Decision-Making, Flexibility, & Comfort Zones

66

"Change begins the moment you get the courage and step outside your comfort zone; change begins at the end of your comfort zone."

-Roy T. Bennett, author of The Light in the Heart

"It is not the strongest of the species that survives, nor the most intelligent. It is the one that is most adaptable to change."

-Charles Darwin, scientist

99

Perfectionism, as you're learning, can impact your life in many ways. It can make it very hard to make decisions and can cause things to take longer. Your comfort zone becomes smaller and more limited, and being flexible can be a real challenge. Let's take a closer look at these three factors.

Decision-Making

Decision-making can be hard when you have perfectionism. Even simple decisions can seem overwhelming, and it can feel hard to figure out which choice to make. Perfectionism can make you feel like every decision is a big one. Decisions ranging from what to eat to what topic to write about to what to wear to what to do for your birthday can all seem like too much; and then the joy of picking out a yummy meal, identifying a topic you are excited to learn about, getting dressed and getting out, and what fun you want to experience on your birthday gets lost for you. Instead, these choices feel like a burden. With perfectionism, it often comes down to not wanting to make a mistake or the "wrong" choice. Also, the longer you struggle with indecisiveness, the harder decision-making becomes in general.

When you are able to make decisions with ease, you become more familiar with your preferences and desires, and you end up knowing yourself better. Also, making decisions easily allows you to be more confident about your decisions. It's a reinforcing cycle—being decisive leads to more decisiveness and confidence in your choices (in the same way that indecisiveness breeds more indecisiveness and gets you stuck in questioning your choices). You learn what it feels like to make a good decision, and at other times if you realize that you didn't make the best choice, it's okay because you will use this information to help you make a better decision next time.

Second-Guessing

Quite often, someone with perfectionism takes so long to arrive at a decision that once they do, they end up second-guessing it. *Was that the right choice? What if this was a bad decision? Maybe I should have picked the other topic; I might not do as well with this one.* In other words, although you picked a choice, the decision doesn't ever really get made—it stays in the questioning and figuring-it-out part of the process. This only makes it harder to make decisions in the future. The goal in fixing this bad habit is twofold:

1. to know and be confident about your preferences, and
2. to practice the skill of decision making in a timely, purposeful way

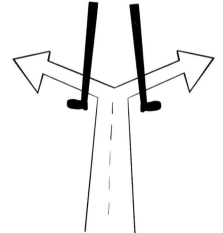

In order to learn how to become a better decision-maker, take a moment to describe who you are, including what you like and gravitate toward. Grab a piece of paper and a pen and answer the following questions:

- What makes you "you"? Describe yourself in a few words. Try not to make it about your achievements, but instead include characteristics that you may or may not be recognized for (your kindness and generosity, empathy for others, how hard-working and driven you are, etc.). Don't overthink it, just write down the first things that pop into your head (no one will be grading this—likely no one will even see it).

- What is your favorite...
  - movie?
  - restaurant?
  - color?
  - sport?
  - book?
  - season?
  - vacation spot?

- Who is your role model?

- What do you want to do when you are an adult?

- What is the one thing you would change about yourself if you could?

- What makes you the proudest about yourself?

- What do you love most about your closest friend(s)?

- What is the most important quality you look for in a friend?

- What is the most important quality you look for in a romantic interest?
- If you had a free day and could do anything, no matter how much it cost, what would it be?
- If you could fix one problem in the world, what would it be?
- If you could live anywhere in the world, where would it be?
- Who makes you laugh the most?
- Would you rather ride a bike, a skateboard, a scooter, or a horse?
- Would you rather be able to talk to land animals, animals that live under the water, or animals that fly?
- If you had to live on a desert island and bring only one food, one drink, one book, and one song to listen to, what would those be?
- What is the most creative thing you have ever done?
- If you could do anything you wanted to do right now at this moment, what would it be?

What did you learn from these questions? Was it easy to answer them, or did it take a long time? If it was easy, that's great; maybe you don't have much trouble making decisions. If it was a challenge, though, it's practices like these that can help. Taking some time to identify your likes, dislikes, opinions, and preferences will help you become a better decision maker. It might help to keep a journal and record your likes, dislikes, and preferences, and log your positive experiences, noting what made them positive and enjoyable. This can serve as a guide for your future decisions. For example, if you made a plan with friends and suggested going on a hike at a state park and it was fun and rewarding, then you know that hikes are a great idea in the future. It may sound basic, but if decision-making is hard for you, doing simple things like keeping a log of it can be a good reminder when you're stuck in the future.

The ability to make a decision is an important skill to have. Ultimately, we want your decisions to reflect your real preferences and values and be a reflection of you. To start, however, the goal is simply to be able to make a decision within a reasonable about of time, and we do this by setting time limits and practicing making decisions this way. For example, if you have trouble deciding what to eat when you go out for a meal, start by giving yourself ten minutes to decide, then the next time give yourself no more than five minutes to decide, eventually getting it down to three minutes. I've practiced with people by pulling up sample menus and using a timer to set the limit. It works! I've also had people tell me that they will decide what to order but when the food comes out, they look at what others around them have ordered and question if they should have ordered that. To help minimize this over-thinking (which undermines your decision), use the following mantra: *It's just lunch. It's just a meal. What I ordered is good enough. I had to pick something to order, and I did it. I'm grateful to have this delicious food.* We've discussed how comparisons with others have nothing to do with you. This is the same idea. It goes back to that pre-school saying of "you get what you get and you don't get upset"; sometimes teens and adults need the same reminder!

When it comes to decision-making, here are three factors to keep in mind:

1. Forget about the idea of a "right choice"; instead, keep your focus on the goal of making a decision. Impose time-limits (use a timer) and remind yourself that most decisions are not going to change your life.

2. Decide on a principle when making a decision, and use it! For example, let's say one of your principles is to be a supportive and encouraging friend. If you are invited to a friend's birthday party but would

rather do something else, you would decide to go the party because it aligns with your principles.

3. Be confident and don't second-guess. Whatever you decide, tell yourself that it was important to make a decision and that you made one. Praise yourself for making a decision. Be confident that you made a good choice in the moment. If you can't stop ruminating over a decision, refer back to the last chapter's tips for worries. The goal here is not to let the decision-making process linger on after the decision has been made.

Procrastination

When decision-making is hard, it can lead to procrastination. With perfectionism, the importance of the task or decision can be magnified, making it feel overwhelming, which can lead to putting it off. When you convince yourself it has to be done 100% perfectly, the task feels like a big mountain to climb. It can even feel like *there's no way I can get all of this done*. Both indecisiveness and procrastination are challenges faced by many perfectionists.

Procrastinators often wait until they *feel like* doing something, but usually that never happens. We often don't feel like studying, writing a paper, cleaning our room, or going on a run. But once we get started, we find that we have the energy for doing it. The motivation only comes after you get started; again, this goes along with the idea that behavior change comes first, and the thoughts-change comes second. Do the action first, then you will think you can do it and it will get done.

Another interesting point about procrastination is the emotional reaction many teens have to it. One study found that students who were able to have self-compassion and be forgiving of themselves when they procrastinated in studying for an exam ended up having less procrastination on their next exam. Self-forgiveness leads to more productivity, likely because it allows you to move beyond the burden and guilt you felt in the past. Also, this shows again how important self-compassion is: it leads to more motivation and lowers psychological stress.

Remember the 80/20 rule from Chapter 4? Another version of this can be used to explain the way we get work done. Basically, it explains that most (about 80%) of the work gets done using only 20% of the time you spend devoted to getting it done. You could study for five hours, but one of those hours (20% of the time you studied) accounted for 80% of all you learned because you were more effective and efficient during that hour. How does this help you when you're a perfectionist? Well, you probably spend way more time than is needed to accomplish something. When you give yourself too much time, like if you tell yourself *I'm going to study all night*, then you will use the whole night to "study" even though only a portion of that time was actually real, productive study time. When you are able to see that the amount of time you spend actually getting something done is a lot less than the whole time you devoted to it, you learn how to refine that time to just the most productive period. This allows you to have more time to do other things, like socializing, self-care, and relaxation. Your life can be lighter and you can feel more free if you have more time, and being more efficient is one way to get more of it!

When you think of the 80/20 rule, try to focus on moments when you are most efficient and most focused on getting something done. Do you work better under time limits? If so, set them for yourself. Also notice when you tend to drag something out; do you usually do this for certain tasks or certain subjects? Does it have to do with how you are thinking about it at the time? Do you feel it will take a long time? Could thinking this way cause you to be slower at doing it? Or is your perfectionism standing in the way of seeing the big picture of what is needed to get something done? Perfectionism can make you obsess over every line of an email to a teacher; you get stuck on writing and re-writing and spend 45 minutes on a three-sentence email. The point of the email is just to ask a question, but you've lost sight of that by over-focusing on how scholarly the email sounds and how it will be perceived by your teacher. Try to use the 80/20 rule as a check for doing the most important parts of a task first and being as efficient as possible so you can enjoy other parts of life.

Flexibility

We discussed being flexible when learning about thinking errors, but it bears more attention. Being flexible can be a real challenge when you have perfectionism. You might insist on doing things in a certain order; for example, having to wake up every morning at 6am to go running for an hour before doing anything else. While exercising at the same time of day is great, when you refuse to change this during a family vacation, or never let yourself sleep in, or won't let a different type of exercise like biking or yoga "count" as your workout, you become locked into what feels like an unchangeable routine. Your family might have to accommodate your schedule (something that many families of perfectionists do in order to avoid creating stress or having conflict) , which only encourages the inflexibility.

Being inflexible often also involves "should" statements. When it comes to school work, you might not be flexible about your rule to check over your work three times before submitting it because someone once told you that checking three times results in no careless mistakes. Socially, you may not agree to plans on Sundays because you spend that day preparing for the week again. Inflexibility makes it hard to adapt and go with the flow.

But when it comes to how you live your life, you are in charge: you can change things up whenever you want. You've created these rules and can change them at any time. Just because you made a rule, it doesn't mean you have to follow it or live by it forever. The same is true when it comes to objects and things in your room: just because you have something or were given something as a gift, it doesn't mean you need to keep it forever. You can decide on most aspects of your life. Challenging your inflexibility by purposely making yourself be flexible is the ticket out of this problem.

Many people struggle with being flexible and need to practice. Here are some of my own examples of being flexible: I prefer not to make a lot of plans on Sundays, but sometimes will schedule myself with three plans in one day. I don't eat meat and am generally a pescatarian (someone who does not eat meat but eats fish), but I occasionally will eat chicken or turkey. I like my room to be clean and organized before going to bed, but a few nights a week I let it be a mess. And (a silly one) purple has been my favorite color for years and I recently decided that my favorite color is actually turquoise! We don't have to fit neatly into a category.

Take a moment to think about areas you are already flexible in and other areas you can work on. Let's go back to the example of needing an email to your teacher to be perfect. Perhaps you are asking a question about an upcoming assignment; you can ask the same question in many different ways:

- Dear Mr. Jones, I hope you are enjoying your day. I had a question about the paper on *Lord of the Flies*, which I am looking forward to writing. My question is: should it be single-or double-spaced? Thank you for your time. Sincerely, Bonnie

- Hi Mr. Jones, Just a quick question: for the paper on Lord of the Flies, should it be single- or double- spaced? Thank you very much, Bonnie

- Mr. Jones, Can you please tell me if the paper is supposed to be single- or double-spaced? Thanks, Bonnie

Keep in mind that Mr. Jones is probably very busy and when he reads your email, he is only reading it to find out what you are emailing about and what he needs to do in his reply back (in this case, letting you know his expectation for spacing). That's it! There is little judgment from others on how you sound or how scholarly your email is. By practicing making your emails short and to the point, and not spending too much time writing them, you will learn there is no need to overthink how it is constructed.

Being flexible and willing to do things differently is an essential aspect of being resilient. It's about being open to new information or a different way of thinking. Flexibility will benefit you in school, socially, and down the road in college, career, and relationships. It allows you to be better at problem-solving and working through challenges. Others will enjoy being around you more; it will take the pressure out of social plans and will make others feel more relaxed when they are working with you on something. If you think there is only one way of doing things, you will not discover how many different paths can lead to the same destination. You will also not discover different paths you may even prefer to take. Like everything else, it takes practice. It will also involve taking a look at what is comfortable for you and what is not; being flexible often requires you to go outside of your comfort zone.

Comfort Zone

What is a comfort zone? It's everything that is comfortable and easy for you, that doesn't create any stress or anxiety. The parts of life that fall within it feel easy, reassuring, and natural for you. Everyone's comfort zone is different, and what may be in one person's comfort zone may be outside of someone else's. For example, some people are more comfortable with taking risks than others. Or, what may feel like taking a risk to one person would not be for another. Taking a risk can be something like trying out for a team, making a comment on somebody's social media page, approaching someone new to talk to, participating in class, submitting your photo in a contest, or applying to be a camp counselor. Whatever it is, taking appropriate risks and putting yourself out there is necessary in order to live a fulfilling life. Perfectionism makes you feel like you are not allowed to fail, and that failure is the worst thing possible because of what it says about you. When you look at taking a chance and all you focus on is what if it doesn't work out, what it will mean to not get it, what people will think, and so on, you are being negative and pessimistic, and this is rooted in perfectionism. When you focus on the idea that it could work out, or that you can give yourself credit for trying, it becomes easier to approach. You may have heard the quote by Wayne Gretzky, one of the greatest hockey players of all time: *You miss 100% of the shots you don't take.*

The reality is that a limited, small comfort zone limits *you*. Not only does it prevent you from trying new things (that you may end up loving), it also prevents you from becoming your best self, feeling confident, and being able to cope with whatever comes your way. The goal is to understand what falls inside your comfort zone and what falls outside of it. It helps to make a list. I like to think of a comfort zone as a circle and picture things either inside or outside of it.

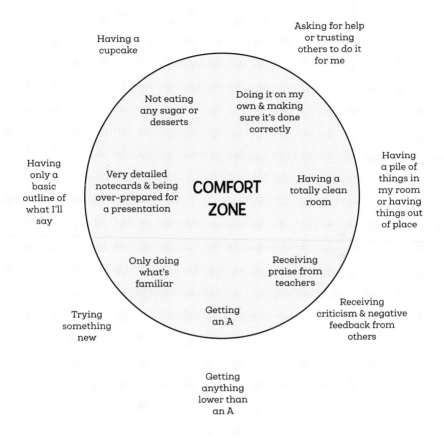

You didn't start out with a small comfort zone: perfectionism shrunk it! For many perfectionists, it's about repairing a shrunken comfort zone— expanding it, making it bigger. When you challenge yourself to do things that are outside of your comfort zone, it will gradually expand, and things that previously felt difficult will become easy and more natural. While it means you will have to tolerate discomfort at first, it will pay off. Your comfort zone will keep expanding as you continue to practice doing the things that are outside of it. It will take a little work, but that hard work will pay off.

Decision-Making, Flexibility, & Comfort Zone Self-Talk:

Here are some self-talk statements you can use if you struggle with decision-making, procrastination, flexibility, and/or a small comfort zone:

- What would someone who is flexible in this situation think? What would they do?
- There are many different ways of doing something. I can try a different way today.
- I am learning to let things go. I can give myself permission to do this.
- Taking action comes first, thinking differently about the task comes second.
- I cannot wait until I feel like it, I just need to do it.
- Remember the 80/20 rule: What is the most important thing for me to do right now?
- How important is this email? Will the person reading it be reading it so thoroughly, or can I get this task done in less time?
- If others can do it, so can I.
- I can take a chance on this. It's good to take risks and put myself out there.
- When I step outside of my comfort zone, it will be hard. Then it will get easier.
- Will this decision matter a year from now?
- I need to face my fears and go for it!

In the next chapter, we will focus on changing your behavior and purposely doing things you would not want to do in order to challenge your perfectionism and limit how much it impacts your life. You will learn specific practices which can help with decision-making, flexibility, and expanding your comfort zone.

Chapter 7
In A Nutshell:

- Indecisiveness and second-guessing come up a lot with perfectionism.

- Learning about yourself and your preferences can help you become a more confident decision-maker.

- When it comes to making a decision, focus on the goal of making the decision itself without getting too caught up in making the right choice.

- When it comes to procrastination, the goal is to just get started (take action) and be efficient, rather than dragging things out.

- Be flexible when it comes to your work and try to not get fixated on how each and every sentence sounds.

- Finally, challenge yourself to go outside of your comfort zone!

Chapter 8

Challenging
Perfectionistic Behavior

66

"The way to feel alive is to change
and to try new things, to stimulate
yourself, to do the things you are
afraid of."

-Natalie Portman, actress

"Being happy doesn't mean that
everything is perfect. It means that
you've decided to look beyond
the imperfections."

-Unknown

99

Challenging your thoughts is key in overcoming perfectionism; it usually accounts
for half of the progress. The other half comes
from challenging your behaviors (this is the
"B" in CBT). Learning about and understanding
perfectionism is not enough; *you must practice
doing things differently* in order to learn that it
is not only okay to do things differently, but
that it is freeing and actually releases you from
the burden perfectionism creates. Making a
"ladder" of practices is the best way to challenge
perfectionistic behaviors. The ladder is a list of

actions you would usually avoid taking. Ladders are also one of the best ways to challenge anxiety and OCD behaviors.

Doing these behavioral "experiments" will help you see there are other ways of doing things, and that these other ways are liberating. Think about creativity: if someone told you what you needed to do, exactly the way you needed to do it, and demanded that you not vary it in any way, your creativity would be squashed. The same is true for your perfectionism: it sets up an ideal goal and you work hard to meet that ideal, rather than allowing yourself the free space to express yourself. This chapter is about figuring out what you need to do behaviorally to challenge your perfectionism.

Exposures

Changing your behavior and learning to tolerate discomfort will contribute to your sense of resilience. Whether your perfectionism is mild or more significant, you will get a lot out of purposely exposing yourself to situations that challenge it. CBT calls this "exposure," and we will set it up in a way where you start out with easier practices and move up to more challenging ones. So, when you create your ladder, you will put the easier steps on the bottom and the harder steps on the top. You are in charge of this process; you are the captain of your ship, and you can always return to your perfectionistic way of doing things. But it's worth a try… and most people find that challenging these behaviors leads to feeling better, less stressed, and lighter. Your relationships will improve, and you will feel more confident. It's amazing to see what happens when you remove the barriers perfectionism creates in your life; suddenly, you'll find yourself without limits.

There are two benefits to purposely practicing, or "exposing," yourself to behaviors that challenge perfectionism. One, you will learn that most situations are not as hard as you expected them to be. And two, you will learn that you can get used to doing things in this different way (even if it's really hard at first), which is called "habituation." Habituation happens when you get used to a thing or situation after staying with it for a long enough time. When these changes happen, your perfectionistic thoughts and the core beliefs that are related to perfectionism will shift as well. That is the relationship between thoughts and behavior. For example, if you believe your excessive studying leads to your good grades, but then you curb the amount of time you spend studying and

still do just as well or close enough, your beliefs
will be shifted.

What's a Good Exposure?

You want to be creative when coming up with
exposures and develop practices that really
challenge perfectionism. For example: Billy had
a strong perfectionistic urge to finish things
once he started them, and would not move on
to the next activity until the previous one was
completely done. It caused problems for him
because sometimes it prevented him from doing
things he wanted to do. One exposure was for
him to get a jigsaw puzzle, work on it until it was
half-way completed, then stop and put it all back
in the box and donate it. When we discussed doing
this, he told me he would "never be able to do it"
and that his desire to complete it was stronger
than his desire to challenge the perfectionism. But
he planned it out: he looked online at pictures of
partially-completed jigsaw puzzles and printed
them out so he could practice looking at them.
He made self-talk cards with statements like:

- It's my choice to spend my time how I want to.
- I don't even like jigsaw puzzles that much. Just because I started one doesn't mean I need to complete it.
- I didn't even need to start it in the first place, so it doesn't matter.
- Many people start things then decide they don't want to do it anymore; so can I.
- I have to challenge these urges to finish everything I start. It is holding me back and I need to switch it up.

When he started to work on the puzzle, he took pictures and emailed it to me, so I could hold him accountable. We discussed that the hardest part was going to be undoing all the pieces and putting them back in the box, undoing all the work and effort he put into it. He decided this would take less than a minute and that he could handle it for less than a minute. And once it was done, it was done. We also talked about flexible ways of thinking about the situation, and he offered: "If I were around someone and they asked me to work on their puzzle for a bit, I would do it and not feel that invested in finishing it. I can just imagine I'm doing that here."

And he did it! He managed to push through his doiscomfort for a minute, pack up the jigsaw puzzle, and donate it. After he donated it, he had a brief moment of discomfort and a harsh inner voice that said *wow, you couldn't complete that, how pathetic* popped up in his head. For a minute he felt a sense of shame and believed the voice. Then he realized this was exactly the same perfectionistic inner critic voice that had popped up in the past, and he reminded himself how much he wanted to get rid of it. It was useful for him to have had that happen, even though it was upsetting, because it allowed him to see his perfectionism clearly and be an observer of it. After this, he tackled about ten more practices of leaving things unfinished, including mowing only part of the lawn and finishing the rest several days later; doing half his birthday thank-you notes and waiting a week to finish them; and putting away a few clothes each day while leaving a partially filled laundry basket in the middle of the room. With his great sense of humor, he would see the basket and say "I see you, laundry. You will sit there until tomorrow. You'll be fine, and so will I." It's actually very helpful to have a playful attitude and approach to the exposures, because this is a serious topic and many perfectionists feel quite attached to their way of doing things. When you can use humor and be light about it, it takes the seriousness down a notch, making it a little easier to do.

I know it can feel scary to do these behavioral experiments. It's not easy and it doesn't feel natural. But when you do it, you won't regret it. When you do it, you will learn more about yourself and your approach to life and how you can shift it. That's a lesson that will stay with you forever. You will become wiser, more mature, and more resilient as a result, and that's worth more than any "A" or compliment or trophy you receive.

Exposure Examples

When building your own ladder, use this list below for ideas (you can also refer back to the symptoms list in Chapter 1):

General Perfectionism Exposures:

- go a day without planning every hour of the day

- have a day without a to-do list written down or in your mind

- leave something partially finished (for example, going to bed without finishing the chapter you are reading)

- explain something without including *every* detail, just the main points

- spontaneously decide you will take the day off from all school work and obligations and do something fun

- try something new (including something you don't think you'll be good at)

- don't correct others when they make a mistake or say something inaccurate

- check things over only once (for example, completing an application for a summer job and checking it only one time)

- re-arrange your room in a messy or out-of-balance way, where things are not in their "right" place

- let someone in your room (ex: to clean/organize your room)

- go with the flow when there is a change of plans

- change your mind

- do a "good enough" job on something

Academics/Achievement Exposures:

- purposely get a 'B' on an assignment

- stop studying by 10pm

- don't ask others about their grades on tests or assignments

- set a shorter time limit for completing an assignment

- spend less time preparing for a presentation or studying for a test

- accept the grade you get (don't challenge the grade or try to get extra points)

- don't stay after class to ask questions

- attend only one teacher study session

- don't email a teacher to ask them about what to focus on for a test

- delegate tasks to others

- only do your part of the work in a group project

- be open to others' ideas when working within a group; don't insist on doing it your way

- ask others for help and guidance (ex: ask someone to read your work and give feedback)

- don't re-do the work of others in a group project

Body Image/Appearance/Social Comparisons Exposures:

- resist comparing yourself to models or athletes

- wear the first outfit you try on (don't keep changing)

- leave the house without makeup or with messy hair

- be on time (don't be late because you've spent an excessive amount of time getting ready)

- skip a work out and watch TV instead

- post a photo of yourself you don't love

- go for a run without measuring the distance or time

- go for a run and stop part-way through the last mile

- compliment someone you think looks great

- try out the 80/20 rule for eating

- wear something tight-fitting even though your stomach is not flat

- admit to your classmates and friends that you were worried about the test and couldn't sleep last night

People-Pleasing Exposures:

- say "no" when someone asks for a favor or makes a request

- ask someone for a favor, one that inconveniences them

- don't go out of your way to help someone or be nice

- express your preferences

- share your opinions when they differ from others

- put yourself first when making plans

- do something that will result in disapproval from others

- ask someone for their opinion or advice, then don't follow it

Decision-Making Exposures:

- pull up three menus and pick out what you will order in three minutes or less for each one

- decide what you will do for your next birthday celebration and who you will invite

- look up three different summer camps or programs, watch the videos, and decide which one you will attend

- send an email in two minutes or less

- ask your parent or sibling to recommend ten different books for you to read, and then pick one

Flexibility Exposures:

- ask your family what they want to eat for dinner or where they want to go out to dinner (instead of telling them your preference)

- do a creative "thank you" for someone without doing a traditional note (for example, write a thank-you poem or make a craft or do a thank-you video)

- vary your bedtime or nighttime routine

- Volunteer when your teacher asks for someone to move their presentation to a different day, even though you had planned to do yours and are ready to go

Comfort Zone Exposures:

- text or Facetime a friend you haven't spoken with for a while

- pick a topic you wouldn't normally choose to write about in class

- apply for a job you don't think you could do, or would even want to do

- agree to go to a crowded concert with your friends, even though you don't like crowds

Sports/Special Interests Exposures:

- take risky shots that you'll likely miss

- let someone take the lead (ex: in sports, pass the ball)

- try out for something you are not likely to get

- try out or audition without preparing in advance

- skip a day of practice (including not practicing your instrument)

- don't take responsibility for an event (for example, if a club you belong to is hosting a charity bake sale, don't offer to bake more than one baked good)

- purposely don't come in first

Relationships Exposures:

- be forgiving when someone makes a mistake or disappoints you

- show understanding when someone cannot do things to your standards, and compliment them anyway

- show compassion to others and be flexible when they do things differently than you

- quickly resolve an argument and say "let's move on and forget about this"

- be the first to apologize and take responsibility for your part

- when someone is running late, immediately reply "no worries, I'm behind too, take your time" even though you are ready

- thank your teachers or coach for being so supportive of you

As you can see from this list, perfectionism causes a lot of avoidance. It's natural to want to avoid something that causes you discomfort or anxiety. However, avoidance only makes things worse. You never end up learning that you can handle it or that it wasn't as bad as you thought it was. You miss the chance to practice tolerating difficult situations and finding your way through them, which is the key to building resiliency. People who have resilience can handle challenges and obstacles, and one cannot become resilient by avoiding things that are hard.

Creating Your Own Exposure Ladder

Now, decide what things you want to do to challenge your perfectionism. Think about things that would be challenging for you to do. You can use examples from the list or come up with your own things—or both! If you have trouble, you can also ask your family members, friends, or teachers to help. For example, you can say: "I'm working on not being as perfectionistic and am wondering if you can give me an example or two of things you've observed that I do because of perfectionism."

If it helps, you can first just list all of the things you do that serve perfectionism, then convert them into "to do" steps for the ladder. Once you've created a list, put it in order from easiest to hardest. Let's say you have 20 items on your list. Number them from 1 (easiest) to 20 (hardest). After doing this, take a blank sheet of paper or a poster board and draw a ladder; in this case, you would draw one with 20 rungs (but leave space to add more rungs in between, since you might come up with more things to add). Then write out each practice in order from lowest number on the bottom rung and highest number on the top. You can also do this on a computer or make it into a checklist, but still list it from easiest to hardest.

Let's go through a couple detailed examples of how it's done:

Kevin was a 16-year-old boy who was a competitive basketball player, and he attended a public high school that was ranked among the best in the state. He was the oldest of three children in his family, and many of the people in his family were professionals (most had gone to college and graduate school). His main stress came from having a lot of anxiety before basketball practices and games, and he would imagine the coach criticizing him and making him do more drills as a punishment. As a result, he was on the quiet side and avoided playing to his ability: he did not take many risky shots and held back from giving it his all. He felt guilty a lot of the time, mostly around schoolwork and grades, and he over-studied to try to alleviate the guilt. He had many friends but didn't join them as much as he wanted, because he felt that he shouldn't have too much fun because it would cause him to not do as well in school.

Though he was always invited and included, he would miss out most of the time and then look at photos on social media of the fun they had that he was not a part of, which led to more negative feelings. At home, he was the first of his siblings to offer to help his parents with cleaning up after meals and chores. He also took recycling quite seriously and felt he was the only one who could rinse the glass jars and other items they recycled well enough, so he would insist on being the one to do it. He also rarely expressed frustration or anger with his parents or siblings, because he didn't want them to be upset with him. Finally, he asked his mom for reassurance continually when he was baking with her; for example, he would ask questions like "Am I mixing it the right way?" "Should I do it like this?" and "Does this look right?" His younger brother even admitted that he often gives Kevin a hard time and Kevin never does anything about it.

When Kevin made his list of perfectionistic behaviors, he came up with 14 items:

- Avoiding talking to Coach Tony
- Being afraid of getting criticism from Coach Tony
- Playing basketball in a safe zone, not taking any 3-point shots, not making any sneaky or aggressive moves

- Arriving extra early to practice and games (usually the first player to arrive)
- Studying too much and staying up until 1 or 2 a.m. the night before exams reviewing
- Spending too much time doing schoolwork and assignments
- Missing out with friends, usually saying "no" when invited or going but leaving early
- Going to parties with my own car so I can leave early
- Looking at social media and feeling like I'm missing out, feeling guilty
- Being the first to offer to help my parents with chores & cleaning up after meals
- Rinsing off all of the recycling items perfectly, not leaving a speck of food
- Rarely expressing the frustration I sometimes feel toward my parents and brother
- Avoiding doing things that could upset my parents, not wanting to make them mad
- Asking for reassurance when baking with Mom so I don't mess it up

After making this list, Kevin converted the items into action steps, and listed 28 practices he could do. Kevin ranked them from 1 (easiest) to 28 (hardest). He did this by going over the list and writing a (1) by the easiest one, then looked it over again and labeled the hardest (28) then looked it over again and filled in the rest of the numbers.

Here is how Kevin's ladder turned out:

Rinse off the recycling but leave little specks of food (14)

Stop studying by 11pm the night before an exam (13)

Stop studying by 12am the night before an exam (12)

Go out with friends and stay out as late as they do (11)

Say "yes" to 4 out of 5 invites for social plans (10)

Initiate a hang out with friends (9)

Don't offer to help with chores or cleaning up after meals (8)

Tell my siblings it's their turn to help with cleaning up (7)

Spend less time on assignments and only revise one time (6)

Spend less time working on homework—set timer (5)

Mix for less time than the recipe says when baking (4)

Bake with mom without asking for reassurance (3)

When my brother annoys me, let him know or tell him to stop (2)

Bake alone (1)

Arrive late to a basketball game & miss being a starter (28)

Ask Coach Tony to tell me three things I can do to improve my game (27)

Arrive late to basketball practice (26)

Break the rules on purpose at home and parents get upset with me (25)

Show frustration toward Mom and Dad (24)

Take 3-point shots and more shots in general at practice & games (23)

Play more aggressively at next game (22)

Tell Coach Tony a funny story from the weekend (21)

Talk to Coach Tony about "The Last Dance" documentary I watched on Michael Jordan, and if he hasn't watched it, recommend it to him (20)

Tell Coach Tony that I hesitate on shooting 3-pointers but I'm going to attempt one in the next game (19)

Let others rinse off the recycling and don't check how well they did it (18)

Arrive on time to practice and only five minutes before game time (17)

Go to party with friends, let them drive or drive them & stay until the end (16)

Be the last to leave a party (15)

Kevin was able to successfully complete his ladder and overcome his perfectionism. It took him several months to do this, but all of his dedication to it really paid off! Here's one more example:

Arya was a 14-year-old girl who would study. Until 1 or 2 in the morning (well past the bedtimes of her parents and many of her friends) and was very competitive with her peers (she talked over and over about this one girl in her grade, Kim, who did better than her by a few points on everything). She said Kim made it seem like she didn't do any studying and often wouldn't want to tell Arya how she did. Kim also did dance at the same dance studio that Arya went to, but Kim was on the "team" whereas Arya just took a few classes. Arya also frequently emailed her teachers to get them to tell her what to focus her studying on, so she would be most prepared for the tests.

This was Arya's ladder:

Once she got to the steps that were higher on the ladder, she needed her parents' help. Every night her parents locked up all her school books and computer in the trunk of the car and hid the key! This was very hard at first—she even confessed to looking up things on her phone to study and that her parents needed to put that in the car as well—but after three weeks, she got used to it. Arya started

Stop studying at 10pm, relax, then go to bed by 11pm (parents lock up laptop)

Stop studying at 10:30, relax, then go to bed by 11pm (parents lock up laptop)

Stop studying at 11:00, relax, then go to bed by 12am

Stop studying at 11:30, relax then go to bed by 12am

Go to bed by 12:30am

When I get a grade that's lower than I'd like, don't challenge it

Plan a social activity the night before a quiz

Get a good grade without telling anyone or seeking praise

Don't ask Kim what she got on a test

Don't ask Kim what she got on an assignment

Don't email a teacher about a test

Only go to one study session

going to bed closer to 11pm and felt more rested. Now, sleeping enough and applying the 80/20 rule, she was spending less time studying and was more efficient. Her advisor at school even helped her plan how much homework time she would need, and it came out to about two hours a night. She also listened to meditation tracks at night (Headspace) and found it very relaxing (we'll talk about that in Chapter 10). Though she wasn't really eager to change her perfectionism at first, by challenging it, she learned that it was manageable. After a few months, she said she wanted to take up the harp (which I thought was amazing since I also love the harp), and she found a music school nearby for her to take weekly lessons. Eventually, she admitted she was happy she challenged her perfectionism, especially before high school, which she knew was going to be more work.

The ladder is so valuable when it comes to challenging your perfectionism. It may be hard at first, but as you keep with it, the steps will feel more conquerable. When you do the practices, you want to *repeat* each step over and over, do it *frequently* (try to do the practices every day or close to it), and stay in the situation for a *long enough time* in order to habituate to it (get used to it). Once you do a step once, put a check or a star on one side of the ladder, and after you've practiced it enough times and it becomes natural or easy for you to do, put another check or star on the other side of the ladder.

Remember that behavior change comes first, and the thoughts change comes second! This is essential to challenging your perfectionism and gaining freedom from it. You can do it!

Chapter 8
In A Nutshell:

- To overcome perfectionism, you must challenge your behavior by doing behavioral "experiments," or exposures to situations you usually avoid (such as making mistakes on purpose).

- The best way to challenge your perfectionism is to build an exposure ladder that relates to your perfectionism. Start with easier things and eventually work up to more difficult exposures.

- Do each exposure often enough and for a long enough time that you get used to it. Once it no longer feels hard, move on to the next exposure. Don't rush it!

- Behavior change happens first, and then your thoughts will change!

Chapter 9

Making Mistakes, Failing, & Life Lessons

> **"** "I've missed more than 9,000 shots in my career. I've lost almost 300 games. Twenty-six times, I've been trusted to take the game winning shot and missed. I've failed over and over and over again in my life. And that is why I succeed."
>
> -Michael Jordan, professional basketball player
>
> "The most resilient people give themselves mental latitude, space to see their setbacks as opportunities to learn and grow. They believe failure is an event, not an identity...in the telling, you recast the setback as a strengthening experience."
>
> -Jena Pincott, Lessons You Won't Learn in School (Psychology Today article) **"**

Perfectionism usually involves a fear of making mistakes or failing that leads to avoiding things because you are afraid of not doing them perfectly enough. Perfectionism makes you think any mistake means *you* are a failure or not smart enough or talented enough. This can make accepting feedback and asking for help very difficult, too. But making mistakes is how we learn and grow.

Making Mistakes

To become a great problem-solver, you must make mistakes. You learn how to be creative when a creative solution is required. Failure makes you grow in countless ways, including teaching you what you are really made of. It can also bring more clarity to what you really want. When we work for something and don't get it, we then learn how much we wanted it or not.

When you are perfectionistic, a mistake might make you feel like you've failed, or are a failure. But making mistakes says nothing about what you're worth. We have to see our worth as separate from what we do or the work we produce or how well we perform (not to mention that how we do varies from day to day, week to week, year to year). When you look at it this way, you won't take it as a personal insult if someone gives you feedback. Even more, how you handle this feedback and how you handle mistakes in general will shape how others see you and think of you. The irony about mistakes is that the way you handle them is more meaningful than the fact that you made the mistake in the first place; your ability to take accountability and cope well says more about you than the mistake itself does. How well you deal with making mistakes also influences how others think of you. When you navigate obstacles and mistakes with confidence and grace, and even a sense of humor, people will admire you for it.

In Carol Dweck's *Mindset* book, she shares a story of a famous football defensive player, Jim Marshall, who ran the wrong way and scored a touchdown for the opposing team. During halftime, he realized this failure would define him in one of two ways: "I realized I had a choice. I could sit in my misery or I could do something about it." He looked at it as an opportunity to do better and recover from the setback. He went back out on the field for the second half of the game and played some of his best football, helping his team win the game. The world learned who he really was through seeing how well he handled his mistake. In fact, I had never even heard of him until I heard of how magnificently he handled a potentially devastating mistake!

Learning how to handle mistakes gracefully is a wonderful skill. When you are graceful and humble, and don't focus on blame or embarrassment, you will see that coping with making mistakes is easier than you thought. When you are perfectionistic, it's easy to assign blame.

Something goes wrong and the first thing you may think is "Who is responsible?" or "Whose fault is it?" Even if it *is* someone's fault, why do you have to blame them? What do you get out of it? How does it feel to be blamed? (Terrible!) As a perfectionist, you may also be quick to blame yourself. If you get a bad grade, you might blame yourself for being stupid or not working hard enough. Blaming involves a harshness that makes you or others feel terrible. This is not an admirable way to be.

I have a funny story: when my oldest son was 4 years old, we drove to Baltimore for the day to go the B&O Train Museum (we live about 45 minutes away from Baltimore). As we were driving on the highway and just approaching the city, in view of the city's skyline, my son said, "Um, where are my shoes?" My husband said to me, "You didn't bring his shoes?" to which I replied, "Why didn't *you* bring them?" Then we had a little back and forth trying to recall who brought him in the car, who buckled him in, and so on. Of course, none of this mattered because we were 40 minutes from home and not turning around to go back. Also, this discussion did nothing in terms of solving the problem. Then I called us out on it: "Who cares whose fault it is? Who cares who is to blame? It doesn't matter. We just need to stop at the Harbor and I'll run in and get him some shoes." Even if it was my fault, or his fault, it doesn't matter. We all make mistakes, we all forget things (even our son's shoes!), and we all overlook the details sometimes. The only effort needed was the effort it took (which was quite little) to get shoes and go on with our museum adventure. Blaming gets us nowhere; it only results in someone feeling bad and puts a wedge in a relationship. It's better to just focus on what you need to do to resolve the problem and how to make the best of the situation.

Getting Stuck on Mistakes

When you make a mistake, it's tempting to ruminate on it, going over it again and again, perhaps thinking about what you could have done differently to have prevented it, or just over and over because your mind can't let it go. It's important to break this cycle, because ruminating doesn't help you at all and makes you feel pretty bad. We talked about writing out and recording your worries and ruminations in Chapter 6, so you may already be using this strategy. If you are ruminating on mistakes or failures, try the following to break the cycle:

1. Write down what happened: write or type out exactly what the mistake or failure was, and provide as many details as possible. Make sure to include how it made you feel and how you are feeling now. Add in any other thoughts that may be related to this one, such as if it brought up past events or other times you felt this way.

2. Read it to someone—a parent, trusted friend, or just out loud to yourself. Notice if your perspective changes as someone else (even if it's just you as the listener) hears it. Do you notice that it sounds different? The goal is to shift the way you hear your thoughts and then shift to different thoughts that are kinder and more balanced. When you become an observer of your thoughts, it changes how you experience them.

3. Prompt yourself: "How would someone who is flexible think about this situation? What would someone who is confident think about this situation? What would I say to a friend who had this experience? Can I let this go and move on?" Write down the way you'd like to think about the situation.

Generate additional replacement thoughts, making sure to include self-compassion.

4. If you are still ruminating, try recording these thoughts and playing them back to yourself over and over until you become bored by the thoughts, and they no longer make you upset (you can do this as a loop recording, described in Chapter 6).

Learning to Fail

When you fear failing, you are less likely to take risks. But failure, as it turns out, is a necessary experience for being successful in life. If you don't fail and make mistakes, you will not learn how to develop grit or resilience. You may not discover what you can do or accomplish by just trying something out and sticking with it, even when it doesn't come easily at first. If your environment works hard to prevent you from failing or making mistakes, you will not learn how to be truly independent and how to rely on yourself. Sometimes it's a loving parent who makes sure you don't fail or mess up at all. While their intentions are good, the impact is not, as it prevents you from learning how to cope and work through challenges. Moving beyond failures teaches you what you are really about.

When we have social failures and are rejected by others, we learn about ourselves and about others. These are invaluable life lessons. We learn who is worthy of our friendship or romantic relationship and who is not. When we are rejected by others, we become more sensitive and empathic, and sensitivity and empathy make you better at relationships in adulthood. I will forever be grateful to my college boyfriend who broke my heart and taught me to have empathy for everyone else who has ever gone through a heartbreak; it made me a better person and a better psychologist.

Resilient Thinking

When you have "resilient thinking" you look at obstacles or setbacks and tell yourself they won't stand in the way of you moving forward and being successful. With resilient thinking, giving up is not an option. You keep on keeping on, pressing forward. Perfectionism creates an obstacle, as it minimizes what you feel you can handle. It creates a sense of being "less than," or overwhelming embarrassment from a mistake, and it's easy to feel like you can't handle it. Resilient thinking says *I can handle it. I'm uncomfortable and I can handle it. I can tolerate the disappointment. I won't let this setback define me. I won't let this setback prevent me from moving forward.*

When you have a "growth mindset" and you make a mistake or have a failure, it also prevents you from giving up. You give yourself credit for your efforts. You value your efforts and feel proud of yourself for trying. If you competed in the contest, played in the game, asked someone out on a date, worked incredibly hard on that paper or project, those efforts are yours to be proud of. Those efforts and what you put into it are worth praising yourself for. Regardless of how it turned out, your effort is worth a lot! In the book *Mindset*, Dr. Dweck explains the story of a horse named Seabiscuit who was failing so much that he was almost put to sleep, and his whole team (the jockey, trainer, and owner) was also struggling. Yet, with tremendous effort and determination, they made him into a winner. "Seen through the lens of the growth mindset, these are stories about the transformative power of effort—the power of effort to change your ability and to change you as a person. But filtered through the fixed mindset, it's a great story about three men and a horse, all with deficiencies, who *had* to try very hard." It is effort that makes you a winner in life, not just naturally being good at something.

When you have self-compassion around making mistakes and failing, you show kindness to yourself, are not self-critical, and recognize that everyone makes mistakes and everyone fails. It's part of being human and it doesn't say or mean anything bad about you. You are mindful of how you feel and how the mistake or failure felt to you, but you are accepting of these feelings, and don't try to push them away. Having self-compassion can actually make it easier for you to work on getting better at something; one study showed that self-compassion and accepting personal failures led to more motivation for self-improvement.

Handling Criticism

Teens with perfectionism are often very sensitive to receiving feedback or constructive criticism from others, whether it's from teachers or coaches or parents (all of whom are supposed to help guide teens as they develop) or good friends who feel comfortable giving open feedback as it comes with good intentions. When you receive feedback or constructive criticism, try the following:

1. **Understand the intention of the person giving you the feedback**. Are they trying to help you get better at something? Are they

giving pointers based on lessons they've learned already, trying to save you from the trouble of discovering these lessons on your own? Are they trying to work through a rough spot in your relationship with them, trying to get closer to you?

2. **Tell yourself you can handle this**. Even if the feedback is hard to hear, you can hear it. You can manage the discomfort. Stay with and practice tolerating the discomfort. Remind yourself that you're doing this for a reason: you want to be able to handle your emotions, even the hard ones.

3. **Consider how you can benefit from this feedback**. When you look at the situation from the perspective of your ego, you are likely to feel insulted. It's easy to get defensive and be uncomfortable when hearing what could be wrong with your work or with your approach to doing something. We can get stuck in those bad feelings and never get the opportunity to learn about ourselves, grow, and become even better. When we recognize that we are all human and not going to do everything right, we can accept feedback not as

criticism, but as an opportunity to get better. Growth mindset!

4. **Express your gratitude (sincerely) for their feedback**. Trust that their intentions are good (and even if they are not, you will have handled yourself with grace and maturity). Try saying something like, "Thank you for sharing this. This is very helpful," "Thank you for pointing this out, because I can't get better without knowing what I need to improve," or "I'm so happy you were able to share this with me. I really appreciate it." Even though it might not be natural to say these things, try it out (remember, behavior change comes first!). With repeated practice, these statements will roll off your tongue naturally and you will start to feel really proud of yourself for being someone who can handle things like this so well.

Learning to Ask for Help

Related to this is the idea of asking questions and asking others for help. Many perfectionists are hesitant to ask questions or ask for help because they view it as a sign of inferiority or weakness. But how do you feel when others ask you for help? Most likely, it is a positive experience for you; it makes you feel confident and good about being helpful, and you probably don't assume they are inferior for asking. It's the same for others who are helpful to you: it will inspire confidence in them. Also, if you ask, you will come across as humble, which is an admirable trait. Finally, when you ask for help you will learn something, which makes you smarter and more knowledgeable. If you don't judge yourself and are not worried about what others will think, you'll find that when you ask for help you gain something, both in feeling more connected to others and learning more.

Asking for help is an opportunity to grow. You are not expected to know everything, and the wisest people know this—they know what they don't know! When you seek answers, approach others for help and guidance, and are open to learning from others, you not only become smarter and wiser, but you grow more connected to others. It's time to view asking for help as a positive thing, a sign of strength (not weakness).

Blessings in Disguise

Many times in life we find that a perceived failure leads to something good. There may be times when something didn't work out in your favor, or the way you had hoped, and you end up discovering something new—maybe something even better. There are so many great examples of this, from ending up at a college which wasn't at the top of your list and discovering it was an amazing fit for you, to going through a tough breakup only to find out you were better matched with someone else, to getting fired from a job and then starting your own successful business. We never know where life will take us, and we never know which "failures" will actually turn out to be blessings in disguise.

When I was in graduate school, I only applied to very competitive pre-doctoral internships. It was a match system, meaning that you applied and if you interviewed at a program, you could rank them in the order of your preference; then the program ranked the interviewees in order of their preference. On match day, to my great surprise, I found out I did NOT match! It was the first real "failure" I had in my academic career: I got to go to my first-choice college, and my first choice for both of my graduate schools for psychology, and I also got to do training at some top hospitals, all of which worked out well. Not matching for my internship was shocking and a major disappointment to me. I felt very ungrounded and lost. I had worked so hard to get to this point, only to end up without a match. So, I participated in what was called a "clearinghouse" process, where all of the programs that didn't match with enough applicants and all of the students who didn't match with a program participate in a second process of interviews. I was very lucky to match in the clearinghouse with a program I hadn't even considered. Little did I know at the time, but the training and supervision I received there was truly the best, and really shaped me as a psychologist. I also got to work with adults there (something not offered at the other programs to which I'd applied), which was very useful, as half of the clients I see at my office now are adults. I also made lasting relationships with my supervisors and got to have an extra year in Chicago (my favorite city) before moving back to Maryland to get married and start my career. At the time, the disappointment was overwhelming, but looking back, it really was a blessing in disguise. There were so many wonderful things that came from that experience, all of which came out of a "failure."

Several people I've talked to have similar stories. One was Jake, who tried out for the varsity basketball team in 9th grade and didn't make it, though two of his close friends, also in 9th grade, did. The coach explained that he only takes two freshmen and then recommended he try out for the

junior varsity team. Jake felt embarrassed and said he wished he never tried out in the first place. After playing on elite teams outside of school since he was eight years old, he felt it was an insult to his ability, and meant he had failed. I suggested he try out just to challenge his perfectionism. He agreed and tried out and made the junior varsity team, which was mostly 9th and some 10th graders. How did his season go? Well, he started in every game, had a lot of playing time, improved his skills, and made many new friends. He also got MVP for the season! Meanwhile, his two friends who made the varsity team got very little playing time throughout the season and spent most of their time on the bench. One of his friends even commented, "You made the right decision to pick junior varsity." Jake thought this comment was funny, because his experience was that he got *stuck* on junior varsity, whereas his friend saw it as if Jake chose it! It was like his friend never questioned what a great basketball player he was.

Another example was Jasmine. In 7th grade, she tried out for a play with a theater company that was known for putting on amazing productions. Play practice was every day after school and every Saturday for three months until the production weeks, which ran for two weekends. Once you committed to it, it was about 3 ½ months of your life where you needed to put the play first. Jasmine had the most beautiful voice and had taken singing lessons for many years. She was also very outgoing and not shy, so it seemed natural that she would do theater. Jasmine went to the audition and tried out for the lead or second lead in the next play, Mary Poppins. She gave it her all and was pleased with how it went. Then they posted the list of who got into the play and what role they would have. She was assigned two different roles: the "bird woman" and a "sweeper." Each role was minor: as the bird woman, she sat there while the lead sang a song, and as the sweeper, she danced with a broom and sang back up to the male lead who sang "Chim chim cher-ee". When Jasmine saw her role assignments, she said she would not do the play! Her mom agreed, saying it was too much effort to go there six days a week for three months for such a small part. Separately, I talked to her mom about why it was so important to get her to do this, and how essential it was to help her with her perfectionism. Her mom totally got it and was on board. I really pushed Jasmine to see that she needed an experience like this to challenge her perfectionism. She ended up doing it, not exactly 100% excited at first, but willing to try. How did it go? Jasmine *LOVED* the play! She loved all parts of it; she sang Mary Poppins tunes all day long, told me she loved hearing the others sing, and that in the end, she cared far less about the roles she was given and far more about how much she enjoyed being a part of it. She also made several new friends and was proud of herself for not giving up on it.

The next part isn't as important as the fact that she did it, challenged her perfectionism, and enjoyed it, but I will share it anyway: after loving this play so much, Jasmine decided to do the next production, which was Shrek. At the audition, she told the director she was happy with any role and only half-jokingly said she felt a connection with Princess Fiona. Before the list was posted, the director called her. During the call, the director explained that she was given the role of Princess Fiona, but she also wanted to explain something Jasmine didn't know about the production company. The director shared that she never lets anyone new to the company star in a leading role, explaining, "in my company, you have to prove that you love theater—and honor all parts of a production—and that you value each role, because a successful production isn't the result of the lead, but the result of the collective effort of everyone involved. Once you get that, then I'm open to putting you in a lead role, assuming you have the drive and the talent, and I now know you have both." Jasmine said it was one of the most important lessons of her life, and one of the most powerful things anyone had ever said to her.

Jake and Jasmine both thought they had failed at first. But they stuck with it and took a risk, without knowing how it would turn out. They learned a lot about themselves, and even discovered that taking risks and accepting something they initially thought of as "less than" proved to be excellent. They learned, before the positive outcome, that taking risks was something they could do. When you worry about failing and feel like failing is unacceptable, risks become scary. When you are not afraid of failure or rejection, and just go for it, you will find that you can handle it and that you get a lot more out of life.

We never know how things will turn out, especially if perfectionism gets in the way

■ ■ ■ ■ ■ ■ ■

If you have time, watch Jia Jiang's Ted Talk entitled "100 Days of Rejection" and if inspired, maybe do your own rejection challenge. This fits with the idea of the ladder and facing things head on, to see that you can handle it!

■ ■ ■ ■ ■ ■ ■

of trying new things, being flexible, and taking risks. Failures might be blessings in disguise. Mistakes might teach you something you never knew about yourself. We can't let past mistakes and failures prevent us from trying new things. We can't keep our comfort zone small.

At first, mistakes and failures can be very unsettling. But it's important to keep in mind that they are needed for growth and success. The next time something doesn't work out as you had hoped or expected, or the next time you make a mistake, remember what you just learned here. Remind yourself *I need this to be really great in life!*

Can You Add to Your Ladder?

If making mistakes is hard for you, or you feel like you don't handle failure all that well, add several steps to your exposure ladder that are about practicing mistakes or trying things you may fail at. You can use some of these examples or come up with your own.

- Do a complicated analytical puzzle or a very challenging jigsaw puzzle. This will help you learn how to tolerate frustration and things not coming easily, and develop more grit.
- Hand in a partially completed homework assignment (to get a lower grade).

- Ask someone for help (you can even phrase it as a compliment: "You are so skilled at chess, do you think you could teach me how to be better at it?").

- Give an incorrect answer during class.

- Send a text to the wrong person.

- Cook something and leave out a key ingredient, then serve it to your family or friends anyway, explaining that even though you forgot the _____ (ingredient), you spent a lot of time on it and hope they still love it.

- The next time something goes wrong at home or with friends, take full responsibility for it (even if it had nothing to do with you). For example, if the milk was left out and now needs to be thrown out, say "I'm pretty sure I was the last one to use it. I'm sorry, it was my fault."

Chapter 9
In A Nutshell:

- You need to be able to tolerate making mistakes. Failure helps you grow and actually contributes to your success.

- The growth mindset is useful here as it helps you see failure and mistakes in a positive light.

- Handling criticism and being able to accept feedback from others without falling apart is important; remind yourself that you can handle it!

- Many times, a perceived failure or not getting what you want is actually a blessing in disguise and leads to something even better.

- Consider adding making mistakes to your ladder.

Chapter 10

Relaxing the Body: Mastering Self-Care

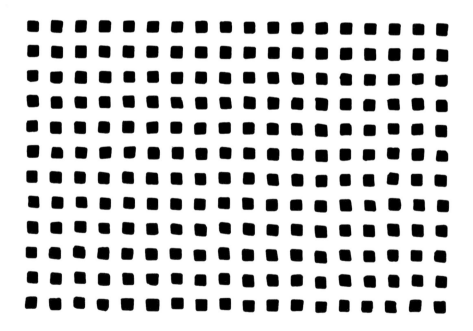

66

"Mindfulness brings us back to the present moment and provides the type of balanced awareness that forms the foundation of self-compassion."

-Dr. Kristin Neff, author of Self-Compassion: The Proven Power of Being Kind to Yourself

99

And finally, the third part of CBT: the body and feelings. Too many people see rest and relaxation as wasted time. Perfectionists are especially prone to this. Why spend time doing nothing when there is so much to get done? But the truth is, you're not doing nothing! You're taking care of yourself—and you can't function at your best when you *do* need to get things done if you aren't taking care of yourself. The goal of learning relaxation and ways of calming the body (and the mind as well) is twofold:

- to address the symptoms of stress and anxiety resulting from the perfectionism that impacts your physical state, and

- to emphasize the importance of taking time out of your schedule to tend to your body and health (which on its own will reduce your perfectionism).

In this chapter, you will learn different ways to relax. Learning the skills and then continuing to practice will take some time, but it will be worth the effort. Taking time to relax and restore (a crucial part of self-care) is often a skill many people need to practice. While some people are really good about listening to their bodies—for example, when they are tired and they just get in bed on time—others push themselves past their natural limit and skimp on sleep, overriding their body's messages (we'll talk more about sleep and the effects of sleep deprivation in the next chapter). It's possible that you might not know how it feels to truly let go and be relaxed, and that's okay, because this chapter will show you how. Self-care is about taking the time to nurture and tend to yourself. Relaxation is an important part of self-care. Rather than viewing it as a waste of time or seeing it as unproductive, it's important to feel proud of yourself for devoting the effort to give your body what it needs to be its best.

Try to reframe it as a necessity, not something you can do without.

We'll start with four different techniques that have been shown to help reduce stress and anxiety:

- Lower diaphragmatic breathing
- Scanning your body
- Guided imagery
- Mindfulness & meditation

Lower Diaphragmatic Breathing

By calming your breath, you create a sense of calmness and relaxation in your body. When you breathe slowly, it allows for more oxygen in the body and sends a message to the brain to relax. This is part of the mind-body connection. When you breathe in a relaxed way, the breath goes down to your lower abdomen, without causing your chest to rise—this is lower diaphragmatic breathing. To practice, try lying down on the floor while placing a book on your chest. Slowly breathe in through your nose and out through your mouth while keeping the book still. You want the air to make your lower belly rise, then as you exhale, the lower belly will flatten. Make sure it's very slowly in and very slowly out, and try to make the "out" breath a little longer than the "in" breath. Do this over and over, until you've mastered keeping the book still and your body feels relaxed and loose.

If you are stressed, your breathing usually reflects that with quick, shallow breaths that only go into your upper chest and don't reach the lower belly. When you are regularly breathing into your upper chest, you might feel chest pain or even get a stomachache. This is a sign you need to practice lower diaphragmatic breathing. It is a good idea to check in with your breathing regularly, like once an hour on the hour, to make sure you are not automatically breathing into your upper chest.

Breathe

Another calm breathing technique is called "one-nostril breathing" which is when you hold one nostril closed, and, while keeping your mouth closed, breathe in and out of just one nostril. Again, it should be very slowly in and slowly out, with the "out" breath lasting longer. Try counting in for 7 and out for 10, and breathing this way for several minutes. One-nostril breathing is a favorite for many people I know! When you do this technique, you don't have to focus as much on your chest or lower belly; rather, stay focused on only breathing slowly in and out through one nostril (with your other nostril and mouth closed). I encourage you to pause right now and take a few minutes to try this method of calm breathing. Do you feel any calmer afterwards?

Scanning Your Body

Doing a "body scan" can really help you release tight muscles. It doesn't take long at all and can easily be done anywhere. Starting with the top of your head and then moving all the way down to bottom of your feet, focus on each different section and purposely "let go" of any tension in each part. Once you do this practice regularly, it will become easy to just notice tension spots and immediately let that area relax.

You can find guided body scans online or in apps, but here's a basic one:

1. Find a comfortable seated position.
2. Starting with the top of your head, sense and feel (without touching) the top of your head and notice how light it feels.
3. Moving down into your head, release any tightness in your forehead.
4. Now let your jaw fall slightly open. Move it gently side to side.
5. Allow your throat to loosen.
6. Let your shoulders drop down toward the floor.
7. Now release any tension you are holding in your chest.
8. Relax your arms, letting them hang loose.
9. Moving down to your stomach, release any tension there. Take a deep breath and let your abdomen relax.
10. Now moving down to your thighs, let them go heavy and loose.
11. Allow your calf muscles to be loose.
12. Finally, going down into your feet, let the muscles release. Feel the support of the floor beneath the bottoms of your feet. Let it ground you.
13. Now scan your body one more time, noticing any areas of tightness or tension, and allow those areas to release.

Another form of scanning your body is to imagine a wash of light—it can be any color you like, preferably a color that is soothing to you—moving through your body and releasing tension as it goes. Imagine that the light, with its soothing, calming, and healing energy coming in through the crown of your head, travels behind your forehead and eyes, all the way down to your jaw, releasing any tension there, then down your neck, and into your chest, shoulders, arms, hands, and fingers. Then the light travels into your stomach, lower stomach, hips, thighs, knees, calves, lower legs, ankles, feet, and toes, where it exits. As the light moves through your body, allow it to take any tension with it, leaving your body completely calm and completely relaxed.

The amazing thing about doing something like this is how effectively you can create a relaxed, calm response in your body in just a few minutes. Even taking three to five minutes to do one of these practices can really restore and reset your energy.

Guided Imagery

Apps will be your go-to resource for this, as there are so many wonderful options for guided imagery (and meditation) available (see the list toward the end of the chapter; my favorite is Insight Timer). The goal here is to close your eyes and listen to a relaxing scene, imagining that you are there.

Take in all of the sights and sounds, the colors and smells, imagining yourself completely immersed in the experience. How does it feel to be there? Allow yourself to be in that scene for as long as you'd like. After you are done, notice how your body relaxed during this practice.

Another option is to recall your own most relaxing place. It can be a place from the past (maybe a summer camp) or a place you are able to visit now. It should be a place where you feel happy and free of stress. Close your eyes and imagine yourself in that place. Again, focus on all the senses and notice all the details of what you see, what sounds you hear, how your body feels in this place. Find a place in the scene to sit or lie down, really soaking up the feelings of calmness from being there.

When you set aside the time to do this, you may be surprised at how effective it is at creating a sense of calm. When you set your mind to being in a scene, it becomes a restorative experience, and it's as simple as closing your eyes and devoting some time to doing the practice.

Mindfulness & Meditation

Mindfulness is when you are in the present moment and fully aware of what is going on in your body and in your surroundings. In this state, you can acknowledge your feelings with acceptance and calmness. The goal is to just stay in the noticing, without judging what comes up. Practicing being in this state builds up your ability to tolerate emotions, even uncomfortable ones such as disappointment.

There are many different types of meditation, but I will describe "awareness meditation." This is where you suspend your thinking and just enter into a state of awareness and being. Take a moment and close your eyes, just trying to be still and be in "beingness," which just means "being," doing nothing, just sitting there with your eyes closed. Try it for a few minutes, without judging whatever occurs.

What was it like? Did you immediately have thoughts and go into thinking mode? Don't worry if you did, because it's very common. We spend a lot of time thinking, and when you have perfectionism, you probably spend even more time in your own mind, focusing on thoughts. The interesting thing is you were not born that way! You were born into a non-thinking, live-only-in-the-moment state. Babies aren't thinking, they just are. They are always in the moment. And they are super-duper in touch with their bodies. They cry when they are hungry or uncomfortable or have to go to the bathroom. When they are tired, they just fall asleep, no matter where they are. Once we grow up, however, we get more in touch with our minds and more focused on our thoughts.

Entering a mindfulness space allows you to see your thoughts as they arise. From this place of "observer," you can see your thoughts for what they are: only thoughts. When you do a mindfulness or meditation practice and you close your eyes, you might be flooded with all kinds of thoughts. They could be random thoughts, to-do list thoughts, or thoughts that are negative or even self-critical. It can even be that you are thinking about the meditation practice and whether you are doing it right or not. If this happens, practice seeing the thoughts as just thoughts (even judging ones). Stay in your "observer" mode and don't engage with them. Engaging with your thoughts is when you listen to what it is saying—the *content* of the thought—and you get caught up in the details, maybe have an emotional reaction to it, and lose the view of it as just a thought.

Everyone can benefit from suspending their thinking and going into a thoughtless, relaxed state. This means you are not thinking: not thinking about the past, the future, or any worries. It means just being in the present. Being in this state purposely, and for a prolonged period of time, is the basis of meditation. With repeated practice, it will get easier and eventually feel more natural.

Try this practice (you can read it, have it read to you, or make a recording you play back to yourself):

Sit in a quiet location, with your back supported by a chair or the wall. Gently close your eyes and allow your breath to settle. You have nowhere to go and nothing to do and are exactly where you are supposed to be. Start by focusing on your breath and feel your breath as it rises and falls in your lower belly, as you breathe in and out, slowly. Now bring your attention to the sounds and vibrations that are present in the room around you, all while keeping your eyes closed. If any thoughts come up, that's okay, just don't focus on them. The content of your thoughts is constantly changing. Try not to focus on the current content of your thoughts. Just see them as thoughts and let them flow right by you. Keep the focus on the sounds and vibrations around you. Just let yourself notice and stay with the noticing. Stay in this space as long as you can, knowing that the longer you stay in it, the deeper you will go into the state of meditation.

Restorative Practices

It's also important for you to discover what types of things make you feel restored. One day during my first year of going to yoga class, we had a substitute teacher. She said, "I'm going to switch it up from Liz's normal pace for class and do a restorative class." My normal class with Liz was more of a power yoga which made us more flexible and stronger. The substitute guided us from one relaxing pose to another, leaving us in each pose for 15 minutes (let me repeat: 15 minutes!)—a very long time to hold a pose. All of the poses were on the mat, meaning we were lying down; again, this was quite different from the handstands and headstands and tree poses I was used to. During the first pose, I remember having a million thoughts come up. I created "to do" lists in my head, considered what nail polish color I would use later that day, etc. I wasn't really in my body; rather, I was in my mind. The more vigorous poses that Liz put us in required me to be in my body—the poses were strong and I had to focus my attention on holding them. When it came to super relaxing, restorative positions, however, my mind was like *okay, what do we do now*? But after a few of the poses, about 45 minutes into the class, my mind learned to quiet down. I experienced my mind becoming clear of thoughts and suddenly noticed my body releasing its tension. I was calm. *Really* calm. Shortly after that, I learned that the word yoga means "to unite" or "to join," and realized this was a joining of the body and the mind. I also left that class feeling completely calm and, you guessed it, *restored!* If you haven't tried yoga yet, I encourage you to do so. There is a reason why it's been around for over 2,500 years!

Some examples of "restorative practices," in addition to yoga, include:

- Doing art (painting, drawing, sculpture, collage—whatever is art for you!)
- Taking a hot bath
- Valuing doing nothing: lying fallow (fallow means "not being used," like how farmers let fields lie fallow and "recover" for a year or more so they don't deplete all the nutrients in the soil)
- Listening to music
- Reading for pleasure
- Sitting by the beach or a body of water
- Collecting leaves, rocks, seashells
- Flying a kite
- Sitting by a fireplace or a candle
- Walking around outside in the dirt, barefoot, and connecting with the Earth (this is called "Earthing")

Others find more active things to be restorative: running, kayaking, exercising, baking, playing an instrument, building a snowman, gardening, going on a boat, or feeding ducks. It's important that you figure out what is personally restorative to you. If you have no idea, then try one of the activities I listed. Maybe you'll find one that works!

Creating a Practice

There are many apps that make doing relaxation and meditation easy. My personal favorites are Insight Timer and Headspace. Insight Timer has thousands of different guided meditations (they even call it "the largest free library on earth"), and my favorite is by Mooji ("Nothing here but you"). You might also enjoy meditations by Tom Evans and ones on helping you relax before going to sleep by Mary Maddux. Take a look and find an app and tracks you like:

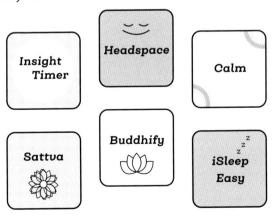

When creating a relaxation or meditation practice, it helps to do it at the same time every day, if possible. A lot of people have told me the only time they have is right before bed, which is an excellent time. Doing a 15-minute practice right before bed can help you fall asleep easily. If you are using it to help relax to fall asleep, then it's a good idea to identify a favorite track and then replay that over and over at bedtime, as that track will become associated with sleepiness. That said, we don't want you on your phone right before bed (it makes falling asleep harder!). I recommend you stay off your phone for an hour before bed, with the exception of the time you are listening to a meditation app (you can keep it on Do Not Disturb during this time and turn the brightness all the way down). Don't look at your phone after the meditation ends (if you're still awake)!

It can also be useful to find a short five to eight minute track to do when you don't have enough time for a longer session. There are even some one and two minute ones! Any amount of time you can set aside for yourself is good, even if it's very short.

We live in a busy, fast-paced world, filled with technology and devices. Now, more than ever in the history of humans, we are bombarded with information and notifications. "Unplugging," even for a short while, can offer your brain and your body a chance to reset. Your brain needs a break from EMFs (electro-magnetic fields) which are in phones and other tech devices. Too much EMF exposure can lead to fatigue, anxiety, and even depression. Time away from it can allow the brain to restore. It can be hard to do, and checking your phone (or whatever device you may use) is very tempting and can be addictive, so set your own limits: When will you unplug? Can you store all devices outside of your room at night? Try it for a week and see how it goes. The main goal here is to make time for getting out of your mind and creating a calmer state; you want to make relaxation or meditation a habit. Once it becomes a habit, it will take no effort to keep it up!

This week, spend some time figuring out what you like to do to relax:

- What do you do to restore yourself?

- What are things you used to love doing when you were little?

- How do you soothe and nurture yourself?

- How do you cope when you are upset, and what resets you?

- Do you like to spend time alone or is it better when you are around family or friends?

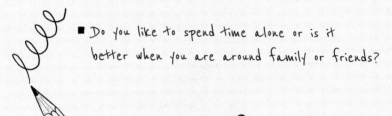

Chapter 10
In A Nutshell:

- Relaxation is a necessity and it's worth putting time aside to relax and restore.

- Learning how to do calm breathing, scan your body, and trying guided imagery and meditation are all ways to help your body (and mind!) relax. There are many apps that can help with this.

- It's important to discover other practices that can help you feel restored.

Chapter 11

Stress Management & Balanced Living

"

"It is not that something different is seen, but that one sees differently."

-Carl Jung, psychoanalyst

"

By now, you know perfectionism causes a great deal of stress and is a barrier to living a full, balanced life. Hopefully you've already begun to make progress in challenging your perfectionism by doing the ladder practices and thinking differently about yourself and all the areas perfectionism can affect: school, sports, extracurricular activities, social life, family relationships, body image, eating, sleeping, exercising, and your ability to relax. Hopefully, you are trying to give yourself permission to be "good enough" at times, loosening your standards and being more flexible. As you do, you can see that not only do things turn out okay, but you are calmer in the process. This chapter will discuss stress management and how to live a balanced life. We want to bring together all of what you have learned and end with a clear plan moving forward.

Improving Your Relationship With Stress

Stress affects everyone. To be human means you will have stress (unless you are a beach bum ☺). Perfectionism causes additional stress and pressure by setting high and unrealistic expectations, having an intensity to your day-to-day activities, needing to have structure, being inflexible, and being critical and hard on yourself. Perfectionism can also cause procrastination, which creates more stress. Perfectionism limits the choices we have, as things need to be done in a certain way, and stress arises when we feel like we don't have options. A small comfort zone means everything outside of it will make you feel stressed. That's why the ladder is so important: it gives you the chance to practice going outside of your comfort zone and trying new things, taking risks, and finding that it all turned out okay.

Stress can also come from social comparisons and social media. Specifically, stress results from feeling a sense of deprivation, which is when you feel like you didn't get something you wanted or things didn't work out the way they should have for you. It's very easy to feel you got the short end of the stick, a raw deal, or that things are not fair. It's easy to look at others and feel like they have it better, which makes it even easier to complain; I remember when, years ago, my colleague and I read this book that challenged you to not complain for 21 days...and we were astonished that we were unable to make it past the afternoon of Day 1 without complaining about something. Years later, when I read more about gratitude and learned how to be a more flexible person, I found it was easier to not complain. I also became attuned to how energy-draining complaining is; it's the opposite of the energy boost that comes from focusing on the good things and what went well.

Finding and cultivating gratitude can be an anti-stress practice. Gratitude is key to being happy. People who report being joyful in life also report practicing gratitude. A gratitude mindset offers protection: it protects you from feeling badly about yourself and your circumstances. No matter how bad the situation or circumstances are, if you look for something to be grateful for, you will find it. Even in the very worst situations, if it caused you to grow or see the world in an expanded way, then you benefitted, and that's the silver lining. Growth is always something to be grateful for.

Cultivating Control

Feeling that you have choices in a situation protects you from stress. In their book, *The Self-Driven Child*, Dr. Bill Stixrud and Ned Johnson talk about the importance of having a sense of control, and refer to not having control as "the most stressful thing in the universe." Think back to the internal locus of control. Perhaps your perfectionism originally started as a way of getting control—creating rules, structure, and working hard to be in charge of your life. At some point, however, the perfectionism became a sticking point and became something that controls *you*. And this is why you are working to get out of it, to *control it*, so it stops controlling you. So, when faced with stress, it's essential that you challenge the perfectionism so it's not in the driver's seat. You are in control of yourself, and in any situation, there is something you can do to change your experience. Figure out what your choices are, and if perfectionism pops up, recognize that it will limit those choices. To prevent this, you need to objectively consider what choices exist for anyone in that situation. It doesn't always mean you can or will change the situation or the outcome, but it might mean you can change how you think about it, which will make you experience it differently.

Let's go through an example: say three of your closest friends were invited to a get-together at another friend's house. You expected to be included but you weren't, and this makes you feel terrible. How will you manage this so your day isn't ruined? What action will you take? Assuming you will not try to get invited or be included, you will have to find a way to cope. If you want to cope with confidence, you might tell your friends something like, "Sounds like fun. Have a great time and let's make a plan for next weekend." Then sometime in the next week, invite them over for the following weekend. You might make other plans for yourself so you don't feel badly that night; maybe it involves getting together with people you don't usually hang out with. Or maybe it involves staying in and watching your favorite movie or playing the piano or learning to draw. The idea is to think differently about it so you are not feeling terrible.

Your self-talk can make all the difference. Try saying things like:

- I won't always do everything with my friends and that's okay.
- Maybe the other person was only allowed to invite three people.
- I'm upset and I can handle it.
- I can have self-compassion and will be kind and nurturing to myself.
- I will not beat myself up trying to find out why I wasn't included.
- I might tell my family or others I am upset, but I will manage this with confidence and grace.
- I know my worth and that I'm fun to be around. I can make this night a good night no matter what my friends are doing.
- Just because they are out and I am not doesn't really matter.

When you support yourself with statements like this, you end up coping better. Again, you might not be able to change the situation, but you can change and improve your experience of it. You might even find you enjoyed the evening a great deal and didn't need to be a part of the plan to have a good time. Or you might discover someone new to hang out with who is more fun than you'd expected.

Let's go through another example: let's say you are co-editor of the school newspaper and one of the articles printed in the most recent edition came out with several errors. It was your job to review the final proofs before sending it out for publication. How do you handle this? How do you think about this in a way so you can cope well and not ruminate on the mistake? One way to cope would be to accept that many newspapers and other publications include errors and the material is still well-understood by the reader (which is the main point of writing something). You might say the following to yourself:

- I made a mistake and didn't read the article thoroughly, but most of the time I do.
- We all make mistakes. Even big newspapers like The Washington Post and The New York Times have a section to clarify mistakes from previous editions.
- I am not perfect, no one is perfect.
- I have a lot going on and am involved with so much, and it's okay if I don't do everything perfectly.
- I have to be okay with making mistakes.
- It wasn't all on me either—both the other student and I missed these errors.
- I will make sure to be more thorough next time, but I need to move on.

- In the big picture of life, this is not a big deal, and it certainly doesn't say anything about me or my abilities as a newspaper editor.
- If anyone mentions the mistake, I will acknowledge it and maybe throw in funny a comment about how it proved I am definitely human.
- If the student who wrote it reaches out to me, I will be supportive and normalize how every newspaper makes mistakes and overall, we have a good record!

If you take this approach with yourself and with others, one that is realistic, flexible, has self-compassion mixed in, without criticism or blame, you will do better in the long run. If you manage your thoughts this way, you will avoid ruminating and will be able to move on, putting your energy into better things (rather than things you cannot change).

Academic Stress

If your perfectionism shows up in your schoolwork and grades, it is important to not only challenge it in the ways we've reviewed in this book, but also to figure out what a balanced academic life looks like. It's the same thing with eating and exercising: too little is not good and neither is too much—it's about striking the right balance.

When it comes to academic stress, here are the goals:

- Stay on top of schoolwork: don't fall behind due to perfectionism or procrastination making it take too long.

- Do not over-study: come up with a reasonable amount of time to spend and stay within those limits. Ask your teacher or counselor for guidance on establishing reasonable homework/study times.

- Prioritize getting enough sleep and having some "down-time" before bed to unwind. Don't skimp on sleep to get more work or studying in.

- Be aware of how much time you spend doing work and socializing. It's important to do both and have a good "work-life balance."

- If you don't do as well as you'd like on something, have self-compassion. Think self-kindness!

- Remember that sometimes it's enough to be good enough. Not everything has to be done to the highest standards.

When it comes to where to put your efforts and work the hardest, pick and choose when and where you want to strive and push yourself, and when and where to let go. Make being flexible your default way of responding. When you have a situation in front of you, think about what it would mean to be flexible and then practice that. Make your mantra: *It's okay for me to do something differently*. When in doubt, be flexible.

Stress and Physical Health

As we've discussed, perfectionism can influence how much you sleep and exercise, and can create a negative relationship with food. All of these factors play a role in stress management. Sleep deprivation is a major problem for teens, and the goal of nine to nine and a half hours per night is rarely met. The consequences are bad for your physical and mental health, as well as cognition, leading to trouble concentrating, irritability, depression, poor eating choices, more accidents, anxiety, and putting the body in a prediabetic state. It's hard to focus and do well academically when you are not rested; it's hard to be able to manage your emotions well when you are not rested. And it's a bad cycle because perfectionism can lead to less sleep. Many teens (and many adults!) convince themselves they can get by just fine with less sleep. Many are stuck in the cycle of sleeping very little and finding ways to get through the day with caffeine or other artificial boosts. But is "getting through the day" how you want to live? What about getting the rest you need, feeling your absolute best both physically and mentally as a result, and thriving? There is an issue in our culture where people take pride in being super busy and not sleeping enough because they are working, staying up and getting so much done, and so on. This sense of being so busy can become one's identity, and the busy-ness may become a bragging point. Being someone with positive energy will inspire others more than being a busy bee who may struggle to "just be." A better source of pride comes from being yourself and living in a balanced way, putting your health and well-being at the top of your priority list, not your grades or other externally-visible accomplishments.

Eating in a balanced way will also help with stress management. Eating whole foods, foods low in sugar, but also indulging at times is the best scenario. Again, challenge the tendency to be all-or-nothing when it comes to food choices. Recognize that enjoying food (including treats) is part of living well. Give yourself permission to indulge every now and then; don't punish yourself if you eat too much or eat unhealthy foods at times.

Make your health and well-being an important consideration when deciding what commitments to make. Make your mantra: *It's not only important for me to prioritize my health, it's necessary. I want to take good care of myself.* When in doubt, say no to commitments that may take too much time away from self-care.

Make a Plan

Now, let's think about your stress management plan and what you will start or stop doing in each of the following categories:

- Time Management
- Sleep
- Exercise
- Nutrition
- Relaxation/Recreation
- Social

Here's an example:

Time Management:

- I will limit my homework time to 4:30-6:00, and stop after dinner.
- I will schedule 15 minutes of listening to a relaxation app before bed.

Sleep:

- No matter what, I will stop everything and get in bed by 11.
- I will tell myself that the kitchen is closed, gym is closed, and library is closed and make myself get in bed.
- I'll take a hot shower right before bed since it makes me tired.
- I'll read for pleasure for 20 minutes before bed.
- I will remind myself that I've never regretted getting a good night's sleep.

Exercise:

- I will work out for 30 minutes five days a week.
- I won't get mad at myself if I miss a day.
- I will be in the moment when I'm exercising and focus on how great it feels.

Nutrition:

- I will stop blaming myself for eating too many carbs.
- I will stop weighing myself.
- I will tell my friends that we need to order dessert every weekend and will have them take a funny picture of me eating it.
- I will stop writing down everything I eat!
- I will savor the foods I eat.

Relaxation/Recreation:

- I will listen to a relaxation app before bed.
- I will go on more walks.
- I will play a game when my family asks.

Social:

- I will have two plans with friends every week.
- I will answer when my friends Facetime me.
- I will not leave early or keep it short.

Your plan may look a lot like this, or it might have some completely different things on it. It might also start with just a few things, and you can slowly add to it. Remember: don't let perfectionism get in the way of starting! It's okay if your plan isn't this thorough at first. It's just important to get started with some things!

Balanced Living

When someone is living their life in a balanced way, with clear goals about what they value, they are free. They figure out what they are passionate about, what brings them joy and satisfaction, and they pursue goals related to these things. They do things they love to do and while they work hard, they focus on well-being as well.

Perfectionism can make you feel like you need to work, work, work, and achieve and accomplish, before you can have fun and enjoy life. But it's okay for happiness to be a goal. When you are happy, you create good energy and your best work will come from this place anyway. I know when I'm in a good mood, my writing flows and is better than if I'm stressed or feel pressured. It's a lot about having an optimistic attitude. When you are positive and believe things will work out for you in life, you will feel optimistic about the future. That optimism charges you with a lot of good feelings.

You have to be able to play, just for the sake of having fun. When you are perfectionistic, it's easy to feel your time needs to be productive. When you measure your self-worth by how much you've accomplished, you end up focusing most of your time on accomplishing things. But our minds and our bodies need time that is not structured, where nothing gets accomplished, where we can wander around and play. When you do this, at first it may feel unnatural, but with practice you will see that it is very rewarding. Notice how it feels to give yourself permission to just be, to just play, and to just have fun, with nothing other than "I played and had fun today" or "I took the day to relax" as what you "accomplished."

Similarly, in balanced living, you focus on what went right, not what went wrong. And even when things go wrong or don't work out in the way you had hoped, you can find gratitude for what you learned. It's important to acknowledge and celebrate what did go well, including your efforts. Celebrate your successes, even small ones, even ones that are stepping-stones to larger ones. When you are positive and strive to feel good about yourself, you enjoy celebrating yourself. This is also related to good self-esteem: when your sense of self-worth is high, celebrating yourself is natural. Good self-esteem allows you to not feel shame when things don't work out or when you fail at something.

Self-Esteem & Healthy Relationships

Recognize both your strengths and weaknesses. We have to accept that we have both. It's not just about valuing what you achieve and accomplish and what you are externally rewarded for; it's about knowing and valuing *who* you are, your character, the warmth you bring to others' lives, the parts of you that make you *you*! If there are people in your life who make you feel badly about yourself or breed self-doubt in you, your self-esteem can be impacted. Spending time with people who are competitive or who are also perfectionistic, or who struggle to be authentic, can make it hard to relax socially. Sometimes others put you down to boost themselves up; you may even find yourself doing the same (even if you don't say it out loud, you might be thinking it). But a boost like this is artificial—it doesn't generate true self-esteem.

Part of creating balance is not letting those types of people in your life, or if they are unavoidable, then minimizing their influence over you by seeing it for what it is, and not buying into it. This is not just for friends and peers, but also for coaches and even people in your extended family. It's important to bring positive influences into your life while minimizing negative forces.

When you surround yourself with people who make you feel good about yourself, who are positive and real, you will feel your best socially. Spend time with others who bring you up, not put you down. And put out positive vibes to others; remember you get back what you give. True self-esteem comes from knowing yourself and valuing your worth for who you are, not based on how you compare to others. Stay true to loving yourself, supporting yourself, and believing in yourself. Be a true friend to yourself.

We also have to have realistic standards when it comes to others and our relationships. Everyone makes mistakes; no one is perfect. To have strong, meaningful relationships, you need to:

- Give others the benefit of the doubt.
- Be forgiving of others.
- Be a positive, encouraging force in others' lives.
- Create a balance between when you bring up a disappointment with someone and when you let it go.

- Avoid being critical and saying critical statements.
- Be understanding and try to see things from their perspective.
- Focus on someone's intent (did they have good intentions in the situation or for you in general?) and not always the impact (how it made you feel).
- Have the goal of working through conflicts and challenges with good communication and a positive outlook.
- Communicate openly with a non-judging tone (a good tip here is to use "I" statements, such as "I felt hurt when you didn't invite me," as this takes the tendency to blame out of it).
- Apologize when you did something wrong OR when the other person's feelings were hurt.
- Take accountability (own what role you had in the conflict) and don't place blame. Remember blaming gets us nowhere, and it's better to put your energies into working on resolving the problem and coming up with creative solutions.

Bringing It All Together

Congratulations: you've reached the end of the book! I am proud of you for reading it and working through these lessons. Self-improvement is not always easy; it's often hard to look at ourselves and figure out what needs to change and then actually make those changes. Many adults struggle with this, too. By now, you have learned about perfectionism and its impact, perfectionistic thoughts and behaviors, and what to do to challenge perfectionism in your life. Hopefully, you have adopted a new way of thinking about things, and have tried out a new way of being, one where perfectionism is not in charge.

We have focused on many different areas perfectionism affects. Moving forward, the goal is to hone in on the areas that have impacted you the most, and let that be the focus on your ladder and your plan. If your perfectionism is mostly academic, use the guidelines from earlier in this chapter, spend your time challenging your thoughts and behavior. If your perfectionism comes out the most in your body image or appearance, then use the advice from Chapter 3 and ensure your behavior and habits around eating and exercise stay balanced to keep up your progress. If perfectionism makes it hard to take risks or put yourself out there, continue to practice your self-talk to push yourself outside of your comfort zone. Even after you have completed your ladder, make sure you continue to prevent perfectionism by keeping up with the behavioral practices. Some call it "exposure lifestyle."

Use this book as a refresher anytime you need it, making sure to get support from parents, friends, and if needed, teachers and coaches. Keeping track of your continuous efforts to challenge thoughts and behaviors will be the best relapse prevention plan, which will protect your freedom from perfectionism. Working through perfectionism takes work, but it's worth it. You can do it!

Chapter 11
In A Nutshell:

- Stress is unavoidable, but your relationship with it will greatly affect your outlook on life.

- You have a choice in how you respond to situations. Try to actively choose to respond in more positive ways.

- Developing positive sleep, eating, and exercise habits will support your health. Create a plan!

- Healthy relationships are essential to feeling your best.

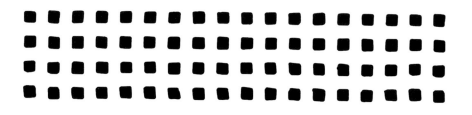

FURTHER READING & RESOURCES

Reading for Teens

Conquer Negative Thinking for Teens: A Workbook to Break the Nine Thought Habits That Are Holding You Back, by Mary Karapetian Alvord and Anne McGrath

The 7 Habits of Highly Effective Teens, by Sean Covey

The Self-Compassion Workbook for Teens: Mindfulness and Compassion Skills to Overcome Self-Criticism and Embrace Who You Are, by Karen Bluth and Kristin Neff

Zero to 60: A Teen's Guide to Manage Frustration, Anger, and Everyday Irritations, by Michael Tompkins

Take Control of OCD: The Ultimate Guide for Kids With OCD, by Bonnie Zucker

Reading for Parents

When Perfect Isn't Good Enough: Strategies for Coping With Perfection, 2nd edition, by Richard P. Swinson and Martin M. Antony

The Gifts of Imperfection: Let Go of Who You Think You're Supposed to Be and Embrace Who You Are, by Brené Brown

Where You Go Is Not Who You'll Be: An Antidote to the College Admissions Mania, by Frank Bruni

Mindset: The New Psychology of Success, by Carol Dweck

What to Say When You Talk to Yourself: Powerful New Techniques to Program Your Potential for Success, by Shad Helmstetter

The Gift of Failure: How the Best Parents Learn to Let Go So Their Children Can Succeed, by Jessica Lahey

13 Things Mentally Strong Parents Don't Do: Raising Self-Assured Children and Training Their Brains for a Life of Happiness, Meaning, and Success, by Amy Morin

Self-Compassion: The Proven Power of Being Kind to Yourself, by Kristin Neff

Eat to Beat Depression and Anxiety: Nourish Your Way to Better Mental Health in Six Weeks, by Drew Ramsey

The Overachievers: The Secret Lives of Driven Kids, by Alexandra Robbins.

The Self-Driven Child: The Science and Sense of Giving Your Kids More Control Over Their Lives, by William Stixrud and Ned Johnson

How Children Succeed: Grit, Curiosity, and the Hidden Power of Character, by Paul Tough

Mobile Apps

Calm

Headspace

Buddhify

Insight Timer

Happy, Not Perfect

iSleep Easy

Sattva

REFERENCES

Chapter 1

Brown, B. (2010). *The gifts of imperfection*. Hazeldon.

Deri, S., Davidai, S., & Gilovich, T. (2017). Home alone: Why people believe others' social lives are richer than their own. *Journal of Personality and Social Psychology, 113*(6), 858-877.

Grant, A. (2018, December 8). What straight-A students get wrong. *The New York Times*, Section SR, pg. 2.

Kemp, J. (2019). Understanding unhelpful perfectionism. *International OCD Foundation OCD Newsletter, 33* (4).

Lewis, K. R. (2014, December). Perfectionism in children. *Washington Parent*.

Stoeber, J. (Ed.). (2018). *The psychology of perfection: Theory, research, applications*. Routledge.

Shahnaz, A., Saffer, B.Y., & Klonsky, D. (2017). The relationship of perfectionism to suicide ideation and attempts in a large online sample. *Personality and Individual Differences, 130*, 117-121.

Sirois, F., & Molnar, D.S. (Eds.). (2016). *Perfectionism, health, & wellbeing*. Springer.

Chapter 2

Bruni, F. (2015). *Where you go is not who you'll be: An antidote to the college admissions mania*. Grand Central Publishing.

Duckworth, A. (2016). *Grit: The power of passion and perseverance*. Scribner.

Dweck, C. (2016). *Mindset: The new psychology of success*. Ballantine Books.

Mischel, W. (2015). *The marshmallow test: Why self-control is the engine of success*. Little, Brown and Company.

Neff, K. (2011). *Self-compassion: The proven power of being kind to yourself*. William Morrow.

Ravenscraft, E. (2019, June 3). Practice ways to improve your confidence (and why you should). *The New York Times*, Section A, pg. 3.

Sanguras, L.Y. (2018). *Raising children with grit: Parenting passionate, persistent, and successful kids*. Prufrock Press.

Stixrud, W. (2018, March 22). It's time to tell your kids it doesn't matter where they go to college. *Time Magazine*.

Stixrud, W., & Johnson, N. (2018). *The self-driven child: The science and sense of giving your kids more control over their lives*. Viking.

van der Kolk, B. (2014). *The body keeps the score: Brain, mind, and body in the healing of trauma*. Viking.

Zander, R.S., & Zander, B. (2002). *The art of possibility: Transforming professional and personal life*. Penguin Books.

Chapter 3

Curren, T., & Hill, A.P. (2019). Perfectionism is increasing over time: A meta-analysis of birth cohort differences from 1989 to 2016. *Psychological Bulletin, 145*(4), 410-429.

Cushman, A. (2007, August 28). The wellspring of joy. *Yoga Journal*.

Deri, S., Davidai, S., & Gilovich, T. (2017). Home alone: Why people believe others' social lives are richer than their own. *Journal of Personality and Social Psychology, 113*(6), 858-877.

Messinger, H. (2019, November 19). Dis-like: How social media feeds into perfectionism. *Penn Medicine News Blog*.

Olsezewski, L.E. (2017, December 20). We need to talk about social media and teen perfectionism. *Mount Sinai Adolescent Health Center blog*.

Riehm, K.E., Feder, K.A., Tormohlen, K.N., et al.

(2019). Associations between time spent using social media and internalizing and externalizing problems among US youth. *JAMA Psychiatry, 76*(12), 1266-1273.

Chapter 4

Natterson, C. (2020). *Decoding boys: New science behind the subtle art of raising sons*. Ballantine Books.

Walsh, J.J., Barnes, J.D., Cameron, J.D., Goldfield, G.S., Chaput, J., Gunnell, K.E., et al. (2018). Associations between 24-hour movement behaviours and global cognition in US children: A cross-sectional observational study. *The Lancet Child & Health*, 2(11), 783-791.

Chapter 5

Egan, S., van Noort, E., Chee, A., Kane, R., Hoiles, K., Shafran, R., & Wade, T. (2014). A randomised controlled trial of face to face versus pure online self-help cognitive behavioural treatment for perfectionism. *Behaviour Research and Therapy, 63*, 107-113.

Kothari, R., Egan, S., Wade, T., Andersson, G., & Shafron. R. (2016). Overcoming perfectionism: Protocol of a randomized controlled trial of internet-based guided self-help cognitive behavioral therapy intervention. *JMIR Research Protocols, 5*(4), e215.

Chapter 6

Antony, M.M., & Swinson, R.P. (2009). *When perfect isn't good enough: Strategies for coping with perfectionism, 2nd edition*. New Harbinger.

Carlson, R. (2006). *You can be happy no matter what: Five principles for keeping life in perspective*. New World Library.

Carnegie, D. (2004). *How to stop worry and start living: Time tested methods for conquering worry*. Gallery Books.

Gittleman, A.L. (2010) *Zapped: Why your cell phone shouldn't be your alarm clock and 1,268 ways to outsmart the hazards of electronic pollution*. HarperOne.

Helmstetter, S. (2017). *What to say when you talk to your self: Powerful new* techniques to program your potential for success. Gallery Books.

Leahy, R. (2006). *The worry cure: Seven steps to stop worry from stopping you*. Harmony.

Wells, A. (2009). *Metacognitive therapy for anxiety and depression*. The Guilford Press.

Chapter 7

Sirois, F. (2012). Procrastination and stress: Exploring the role of self-compassion. *Self & Identity, 13*(2), 128-145.

Wohl, M.J.A., Pychyl, T.A., & Bennett, S.H. (2010). I forgive myself, now I can study: How self-forgiveness for procrastinating can reduce future procrastination. *Personality & Individual Differences, 48*, 803-808.

Chapter 8

Dweck, C. (2016). *Mindset: The new psychology of success*. Ballantine Books.

Chapter 9

Alvord, M.K., & McGrath, A. (2017). *Conquer negative thinking for teens: A*

workbook to break the nine thought habits that are holding you back. New Harbinger.

Breines, J.G., & Chen, S., (2012). Self-compassion increases self-improvement motivation. *Personality & Social Psychology Bulletin, 38*(9), 1133-1143.

Dweck, C. (2016). *Mindset: The new psychology of success*. Ballantine Books.

Pincott, J. (2018, May/June). Lessons you won't learn in school. *Psychology Today*, 51-61.

Chapter 10

NurrieStearns, M. & NurrieStearns, R. (2010). *Yoga for anxiety: Meditations and practices for calming the body and mind*. New Harbinger.

Chapter 11

Stixrud, W., & Johnson, N. (2018). *The self-driven child: The science and sense of giving your kids more control over their lives*. Viking.

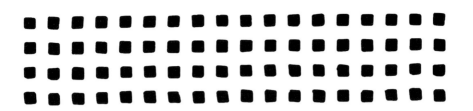

ACKNOWLEDGMENTS

Thank you first and foremost to Kristine Enderle, Editorial Director at Magination Press, for the honor of writing this book and for her flexibility in waiting for me to do it! Working with you over these years has been an absolute pleasure, and a true gift.

Katie Ten Hagen's editorial excellence fully shaped this book into being. Thank you, Katie, for your outstanding guidance and for putting 100% into making this book all it can be for the reader. I am extremely grateful for you!

Everything I have learned about perfectionism comes from my mentors and my clients. A special thank you to Drs. Rudy Bauer, Mary Alvord, Bernie Vittone, and Bill Stixrud for their ongoing influence and for streaming such light into my life. I am forever indebted to my clients, who have let me into their minds and their hearts, and have trusted my guidance: your determination and perseverance on the path to betterment continues to amaze and inspire me.

My associates at Bonnie Zucker & Associates, Drs. Silvi Guerra, Erica Moran Etter, and Anna Pozzatti have supported and cheered me on in countless ways. I am so grateful for our team and so proud of the difference we are making.

Thank you to Brian, my loving and kind husband, for honoring my work and my writing and for his endless support and patience every time I've had to put it first. Thank you to my sweet boys, Isaac and Todd, who at their young ages of 13 and 8, have more wisdom and awareness than I could imagine, and whose love and warmth bring me joy and peace every day. Thank you for encouraging me as I wrote this book, and for being so patient and understanding. Thank you to my wonderful sister-in-law, Lisa Friedlander, for her enthusiasm and good energy, and for always believing in me. And to my Aunt Karen, a constant source of love, you inspire me with your ability to live life authentically and in color: thank you for caring so much about everything I do, especially the books.

If it weren't for my very best friend and sister, Emily Celler, I would not be nearly as flexible, or as fun. Thank you for fostering my confidence, for pushing me outside of my comfort zone time and time again, and for loving me both as R&R and who I am today. Your sisterhood is a gift I treasure always.

Finally, I am eternally grateful for the love and influence of my mother. Without any pressure for or expectation of perfection and with unwavering confidence in me, she encouraged me to follow my dreams, have compassion for others, and was a great model of work-life balance. Moreover, she taught me how to celebrate life.

INDEX

C

D

Recreation, in stress
management plan, 217
Rejection challenge, 183
Relationships
for balanced living, 220–222
in college, 14
comparing vs. connecting
in, 59–60
exposures for, 153
meaningful, 221–222
perfectionism about, 20
Relative comparisons, 58
Relaxing the body, 83,
186–196, 199–203
body scan for, 191–192
breathing techniques for,
189–191
creating a practice for,
199–202
guided imagery for, 192–193
mindfulness and
meditation for, 193–196
and restorative practices,
197–199
in stress management plan,
217
Resilience, 22, 46
and avoidance, 154
and behavior change, 142
from failure or mistakes, 171
for success in life, 39–40
Resilience mindset, 99, 118
Resilient thinking, 172–174
Restorative practices, 197–199
Risks, taking, 136, 183
Rumination/rumination
cycle, 85, 112–115
about mistakes, 169–171
feelings engendered by, 32

S

School, 10–15. *See also*
Academics
Second-guessing, 123–128
Selective attention, 104–106,
110
Self-awareness, 22
Self-blame, 6
Self-care, 68
for balanced living, 218–222
for managing stress. *See*
Stress management
relaxing the body, 187, 188.
See also Relaxing the body

restorative practices,
197–199
Self-compassion, 46
around mistakes and
failures, 174
and self-confidence, 34
in self-talk, 116–117
for success in life, 29–33
Self-Compassion (Neff), 29–30
Self-confidence, 46
and feeling good about
yourself, 77–78
and self-care, 68
self-talk inspiring, 118
for success in life, 33–35
Self-criticism in perfectionism,
6, 20, 25
self-compassion vs., 29
in sports, 15
The Self-Driven Child (Stixrud
and Johnson), 208
Self-efficacy, 46
self-talk reflecting, 118
for success in life, 40–41
Self-esteem, 6
in balanced living, 220–222
self-confidence vs., 34
Self-forgiveness, 129
Self-kindness, 29–32, 77
with mistakes and failures,
174
in self-talk, 117
Self-talk in changing
behaviors, 144–145
in changing thoughts, 93,
95, 100–102, 115–119
in cultivating control,
210–212
for decision-making,
flexibility, and comfort zone,
138
kind, 30, 32
Self-worth
basis of, 166, 219
confidence in, 60
core beliefs about, 111–112
and exercise obsession, 74
self-esteem vs., 34
"Shoulds," 72, 99–101, 106, 132
Sleep, 188, 213–214, 216
Social comparisons
exposures for, 149–150
and focus on appearance, 50
preventing, 58–59